Summarize forecasting and how it is used in HR.

Define job analysis and its primary purpose.

Explain the importance of conducting job analysis.

Explain information collection for use in job analysis.

Describe the job analysis methods of observation,
interview, and behavioral event interview.

Describe the job analysis methods of observation,
interview, and behavioral event interview.

Job analysis involves the systematic evaluation of activities and responsibilities in a specific job. The three main products of a job analysis are job competencies, job specifications, and job descriptions. **Job competencies** are a detailed list of all broad skills and traits needed for a particular position. **Job specifications** are detailed descriptions of all specific qualifications an individual must have to perform the role. A **job description** is a detailed, written breakdown of all tasks that a worker in that role must complete, as well as the job competencies and job specifications required to be qualified for that role. Some of the major uses of job analysis include the following:

- HR planning to develop job categories
- Recruiting to describe and advertise job openings
- Selection to identify skills and criteria for choosing candidates
- Orientation to describe activities and expectations to employees
- Evaluation to identify standards and performance objectives
- Compensation to evaluate job worth and develop pay structures
- Training to conduct needs assessments
- Discipline to correct subpar performance
- Safety to identify working procedures and ensure workers can safely perform duties
- Job redesign to analyze job characteristics that periodically need updating
- Legal protection to identify essential functions that must be performed and safeguard the organization against claims

Forecasting in business is the ability to predict or estimate, based on past data, the likelihood of a particular event becoming a reality. In HR, forecasting is used to predict the staffing needs of an organization as well as the financial impact of all costs related to labor (benefits, training, etc.). HR forecasting can be short- or long-term and is dependent on many factors in an organization, such as revenue, growth, and attrition. Forecasting assists the HR plan for the number and types of employees the organization will need and related costs. Forecasting enables the organization to plan for growth based on educated, quantitative information and also permits the organization to make decisions in the event of downsizing. In addition to using forecasting for direct staffing needs, an organization also uses it for budgeting. For example, forecasting may reveal that an organization needs more employees in the months of November and December. HR must examine its budget and determine if it makes more sense to pay overtime to existing workers, hire temporary workers, or have a small staff of part-time employees.

Job analysis begins with the collection of pertinent information about a particular job. This information can best be described as job characteristics that differentiate a specific job from other jobs. These characteristics may include the following:

- Level of supervision, whether provided or received
- Computer, machine, or other technical equipment used
- External and/or internal interaction
- Specific work activities and behaviors needed
- Knowledge or education needed, sometimes referred to as "knowledge, skills, and abilities" (KSAs)
- Performance standards
- Working conditions

Grouping jobs by similar function is usually advantageous during the job analysis process. This is frequently accomplished by defining the overall job family and drilling down to job responsibilities, then specific details about work performed. For example:

- Job family: HR service center
  - Job: HR call center representative
    - Task: Provides support by phone and/or email for customer inquires

A job analysis is an essential part of any workforce planning process because it identifies specific skills and knowledge required to meet staffing goals and objectives. It also identifies the specific skills and qualifications required to meet the strategic goals and objectives set for the organization as a whole. A job analysis not only allows the organization to identify which tasks need to be performed, but also breaks those tasks into specific skills, traits, and knowledge that would qualify an individual to perform each task appropriately.

The following are some of the most common job analysis methods that can be deployed, depending on a variety of circumstances:

- **Structured questionnaire**—These questionnaires only permit very specific responses to obtain information about the frequency of particular tasks and the importance of the skills required to perform those tasks. This finite data set helps clarify jobs that are challenging to understand, and the data generated from this type of questionnaire lends itself to being easily used for computer modeling analysis.
- **Open-ended questionnaire**—This type of questionnaire is completed by job incumbents and/or manager(s) to determine the KSAs needed for a particular job. This information is then compiled into a summary document of job requirements. This method is useful for most jobs where the information is available.
- **Work diary**—This method involves an employee keeping a record, typically over a period of weeks or months, of the frequency and timing of tasks. The information recorded is analyzed and compiled for the purpose of identifying duties, responsibilities, and trends. This method involves sifting through a tremendous amount of data that may or may not be useful and may be difficult to interpret and keep current.

Collecting information for job analysis can be tricky, and there is no specific formula because it depends on the job and information available. As a general rule, direct observation of the job and work performed, in conjunction with information obtained from previous job holders, is the most useful. However, this information might not always be available, there may be circumstances that make it impossible to collect the data, or the data might not be reliable. The following are some of the most common job analysis methods that can be deployed, depending on a variety of circumstances:

- **Observation**—After someone literally observes the job, a record of job tasks is documented and categorized into the knowledge, skills, and abilities (KSAs) needed to perform the job. This method is best suited for production jobs or short-cycle processes.
- **Interview**—The interviewer asks pre-scripted questions to qualified people in the job or job incumbents with the goal of obtaining KSAs for the job. This method works well with most professional jobs.
- **Behavioral event interview**—This method is called a "competency-based" form of job analysis because it is designed to get behavioral descriptions about how a person performs a given job instead of KSAs. The goal is for the interviewer to get the interviewee to talk about specific stories or occurrences that happened on the job and gather information about their behaviors, thoughts, and actions in real-life situations. This method is used in jobs that may be considered high-stress.

Define the term "job description" and why it is needed.

Discuss why determining the essential functions of a job description is critical for an organization.

Discuss some guidelines to consider when documenting essential functions.

List some of the key components that should be included in a job description.

Define outsourcing and its application as an alternative staffing practice.

Describe how job sharing works in an organization.

Essential functions are documented within a **job description**, detailing what a job applicant unquestionably must be able to do because it is essential to the job. Capturing all essential functions in a job description is important because they are used to determine the legal rights of an employee with a disability under the American with Disabilities Act (ADA). If an employee cannot perform the essential function, even with reasonable accommodations, then that employee is not qualified for the job and cannot be safeguarded from discrimination as outlined in the ADA. In other words, a person cannot bring a disability lawsuit against an employer if the person, due to a disability, could not perform the essential functions as documented in the job description. A job analysis is significant in determining essential functions because if an essential function is not truly an essential function, then the employer cannot exclude a person with a disability from the given position because they cannot perform the function.

A **job description** documents the duties, tasks, and responsibilities for a particular position based on information obtained in a job analysis. More specifically, it provides detailed information about who does a particular job and how the work is to be performed and completed, and it links the work performed to the organization's mission and goals. There are many explanations for why an organization should have job descriptions for all of their positions, including calculating salary levels, performance reviews, initially setting job titles and grades of pay, measure for reasonable accommodations, and recruiting purposes. Job descriptions are also needed for operational purposes such as training and legal compliance obligations, and possibly in the situation when an employee's performance is in question and may need improvement.

There is not a specific template for any job description because it is dependent on the particulars of the job and the organization. However, a job description is usually standardized in appearance in most organizations. The following are some of the most important elements that should be included in a job description:

- Job title.
- Classification (exempt, nonexempt, contractor).
- Date when the job description was written.
- Summary of the job and key objectives.
- Listing of all essential functions, knowledge, skills, and abilities (KSAs). KSAs may or may not be included in essential functions. If not, there should be a separate section for competencies.
- Level of supervision—Whether the role has direct reports (and, if so, how many) or is an individual contributor with no supervisory responsibilities.
- Work environment conditions such as temperature and noise, and physical demands such as bending, sitting, and lifting.
- Hours—The hours to be spent working on-site and remotely; and/or the percentage of travel required, if applicable.
- Education and/or experience required, including college, certifications, and/or number of years of experience in a specific industry or environment.
- Salary range for the position.
- Affirmative action plan and/or equal employment opportunity statement. These are especially necessary if the position is a federal contractor, but are usually common practice.

The following are some guidelines to consider when documenting essential functions for every task:

- Ensure the task is truly a requirement to perform the job.
- Evaluate and determine the frequency and time spent performing a task.
- Evaluate whether not performing the task would be detrimental to the employer.
- Determine whether the task could be redesigned, conducted in a different manner, or altered in a way that doesn't severely compromise the end product or service.
- Decide whether the task could be accomplished by a similar employee.

After drafting a job's essential functions, the employer should carefully consider whether the functions are truly essential or marginal. The words "essential function" are part of a typical job description and should clearly state that those functions are essential to perform the job.

Job sharing is when two or more employees share the job responsibilities of one full-time job, meaning each employee works part-time, with specific work hours differing slightly between those sharing the single job. Most often there are two types of job-sharing scenarios: (1) the twins model, in which two or more employees work seamlessly together on the same project or service; and (2) the island model, in which two or more employees share a job but work independently from one another. Job sharing is an arrangement designed by the employer and employee, and therefore not specifically addressed under the Fair Labor Standards Act (FLSA). Usually, an organization will enter into this type of arrangement with employees to assist in the retention of good employees who need flexibility in their work schedule, and to attract job candidates for other positions by maintaining a workplace that supports a work-life balance. This may help an organization become an employer of choice or achieve a competitive advantage in the marketplace. Job sharing requires excellent communication between those in a twin model scenario because they must be able to function as one. Depending on an employer's benefits policy and federal, state, and local laws, job sharing could decrease benefits costs because neither employee is full-time.

Outsourcing is the practice of hiring a separate third-party business to perform services that were previously performed internally by employees within the organization. The rationale for outsourcing is almost always cost-cutting, but it can also be an avenue to hire expertise that is not within the company or not financially feasible to hire. Additionally, the decision to outsource allows the company to focus on more critical aspects of the business, thereby improving their competitive advantage. There are three different types of outsourcing:

- **Onshore**—The outsourcing vendor is located in the same country as the parent business.
- **Nearshore**—The outsourcing vendor is in a neighboring country to the parent business.
- **Offshore**—The outsourcing vendor is in a country that is usually not near the parent company.

While outsourcing in general has many advantages as a staffing alternative, it also has some disadvantages, such as difficulty managing the third-party vendor and their employees, loss of control and confidentiality, and negative impact on morale (existing employees may worry about job security).

Summarize the concept of phased retirement.

Explain the term "gig economy" and the dynamics of a "gig worker."

Summarize recruiting and the differences between internal, external, and alternative recruiting.

Discuss the recruitment sourcing of active, semi-active, and passive candidates.

Summarize the purpose of a candidate pipeline in recruiting.

Summarize what is meant by the term "social networking."

A **gig economy** is based on the premise that independent freelancers, contractors, or short-term workers can provide services that are less expensive and more efficient for businesses in a free market system. This is a drastic contrast to more traditional employees in a business, who work standard hours with benefits. The term "gig" is often used by musicians or others in the field of performing arts to describe a short-term job. Hence, a **gig worker** is an independent contractor that provides specific services to businesses, performing a specialized service efficiently and thereby reducing cost for the business. A variety of gig workers, such as food deliverers, drivers, shoppers, musicians, IT service technicians, digital sales personnel, and tutors are utilized to perform assignments.

The propagation of gig workers has been driven by several forces, including technology decoupling work from a physical location, businesses reacting more quickly to market forces without the financial burden of traditional employment, and workers desiring work flexibility and independence. However, gig workers must also contend with modest pay (forcing them to perhaps seek multiple jobs); having no benefits; and not being legally classified as employees, meaning income and Social Security taxes are not withheld. Gig workers must buy and maintain whatever is necessary to sustain their particular area of expertise, and must manage the stress of constantly looking for their next gig. Businesses utilizing gig workers should adhere to any federal, state, or local laws regarding compensation and work classification.

Phased retirement is a process that enables an employee to incrementally decrease their full-time working hours and at the same time draw upon retirement benefits like Social Security or a pension. Depending on the situations and applicable laws, this could mean an employee near retirement could possibly work part-time, job share, or use some other method to reduce their working hours. There are several benefits to phased retirement: it helps slowly transition full-time older workers into retirement, provides adequate time to transfer knowledge to remaining employees, and gives HR time to recruit new talent or strategize new talent acquisition.

However, there are also several disadvantages. An employee switching from full-time to part-time can negatively impact the benefits they will receive in the future. For example, if an employee chooses phased retirement and their salary is significantly reduced for a few years before retirement, it could reduce the Social Security benefits the retiree could receive once fully retired. Additionally, many federal, state, and local laws, and also legal compliance issues that vary substantially from state to state, must be considered before an employer can devise a plan for phased retirement.

Recruiting candidates can be categorized into three primary groupings, depending on the level of candidate interest:
- **Active**—Candidates that are fully engaged in the search for a new job. This type of individual could be employed or unemployed, but is energetically seeking new employment.
- **Semi-active**—While not fully engaged in the process of obtaining new employment, a semi-active candidate is open to the idea of a new job if it presents itself and is a better fit than their current position.
- **Passive**—This type of candidate is not looking for new employment. However, a passive candidate might have a particular skill set or experience that is sought by an employer. If a recruiter identifies such an individual, the burden is on the recruiter to convince the individual of the benefits of a new employment opportunity.

Recruiting refers to the strategies and procedures used to identify qualified people for potential employment by an organization, including analyzing job responsibilities, sourcing or finding applicants, and finding the most qualified candidates. In short, recruiting adds new qualified people to an organization in order to fill vacancies for open positions. There are generally three types of recruiting:
- **Internal**—Identifying qualified candidates within an organization for a lateral position, transfer, or promotion to fill a job vacancy. Some of the benefits of internal recruiting include the fact that the person is already familiar with the organization's culture and procedures, the motivation for employees to work harder for a promotion, and reduced organization cost and recruiting efforts.
- **External**—Identifying and locating qualified job applicants outside an organization. There are many benefits to external hiring, including a large applicant pool to select from, new talent with different perspectives or ideas, and the possibility of increasing diversity within an organization.
- **Alternative or other**—This type of recruiting is primarily derived from volunteers, internships, or temporary workers. Sometimes a temporary worker can be promoted to a full-time employee in an organization.

Social networking means connecting with individuals by using social media sites. Social media lets people more efficiently increase their network of contacts. LinkedIn, Facebook, and Twitter/X are very popular for recruiting because they are cost effective, efficient, and quick to reach a large audience of potential job candidates. This is especially important if candidates are needed in different or remote areas of the world. Recruiting over social media also allows the recruiter to examine the potential job candidate in further depth by viewing the candidate's social media presence and learning about the candidate's interests, goals, and personal preferences. Additionally, social media is an excellent way for recruiters to identify candidates not actively looking for new employment, based on search criteria and matches.

Social media is also a powerful communication tool for HR. An organization's presence on numerous platforms helps capture and communicate their culture, which is another means to attract top job applicants. HR should consider an organization's presence on social media and how it influences a prospective job candidate's impression of the organization's values and cultural fit.

The work of a recruiter doesn't start when a manager opens a job requisition. Just like sales professionals should always be selling, recruiters should always be recruiting. That's how a talent acquisition professional can build a strong **candidate pipeline**.

A candidate pipeline is made up of individuals who may be interested in joining a company when a suitable role becomes available. For example, a recruiter who works for a call center may continuously accept applications and conduct screening interviews for call center representatives, even when there are no jobs available.

Because this talent pipeline is in place, the recruiter will have a head start when the company needs to staff up for a new project or fill vacancies due to turnover. Rather than having to quickly post a job and filter through a lot of applications, the recruiter can reach out to people already in the talent pipeline. They're already prequalified, so they can immediately be scheduled to interview with the hiring manager.

Describe the importance of an employer's brand and the factors that affect it.

Describe employee referrals and how they can be leveraged in recruiting.

Summarize the advantages of job fair recruiting.

Describe recruitment advertising and its primary purpose.

Briefly explain the various formats for online recruitment advertising.

Explain why and how word of mouth could be a desired method of recruitment.

An **employee referral** is a recruiting method within an organization whereby existing employees identify and recommend friends or colleagues in their network for job openings. This is usually a documented program that encourages employees to recommend qualified people they know for job openings. These formal programs usually specify how long the referred person needs to remain employed and who is eligible to participate in a referral program. Additionally, the employee who made the referral is frequently monetarily rewarded or recognized for placing a qualified person within the organization. There are many benefits for an organization to have an employee referral program:

- Employees know their organization and who would or would not be a good cultural fit.
- It is a win-win for the applicant because sourcing through an employee referral program could enable a job applicant to stand out more, placing the applicant in a better position for an interview or other type of screening.
- It costs significantly less than most other forms of recruiting and saves time sourcing a candidate.
- It is one of the ways recruiters can reach qualified passive candidates, especially for hard-to-find jobs.

Employer branding is a very important aspect of talent acquisition. A company's **employer brand** is the perception that employees and potential applicants have regarding what it's like to work for the company. In other words, it's an organization's reputation as an employer.

Employer brand is based on a variety of factors, including:
- What current and former employees say about their experience
- The ease of finding openings and applying for employment
- How candidates are treated during the screening process
- Pay and benefits, in relation to what other similar employers offer
- The company's reputation and standing in the community and industry

A company looking to successfully recruit and retain top talent should strive to be perceived as an **employer of choice** in its industry or geographic area.

Recruitment advertising is a method used by organizations to attract candidates for the purpose of talent acquisition, both for the present and the future. Recruitment advertising can help an organization of any size reach potential candidates across almost all industries and levels of experience. This method of advertising can reach active job seekers as well as passive candidates whose interest in an organization may have been piqued by an advertisement. Traditional advertising for recruitment on TV, radio, and newspapers is still used, but is severely limited in its ability to reach a larger audience when compared with web-based recruitment advertising. Online web-based advertising on general job boards, niche job boards, social networks, and more, is usually the preferred method for organizations to recruit candidates for immediate job openings, and it motivates candidates to learn more about the company, thereby developing a potential talent pipeline. Remember, while recruitment advertising is a method most organizations deploy to attract talent, it is rarely the only tool an organization will utilize for talent acquisition.

Job fairs are used as a recruitment tool to reach a large audience of job seekers in one location. Job fairs can be narrow in scope and size, such as on a college campus; or broader and larger, like in a large convention center. Larger job fairs can be expected to attract a larger variety of potential job candidates. Some job fairs can also be industry-specific. Generally, job fairs tend to be excellent recruiting opportunities for entry-level positions, college graduates, and veterans. They can also be a great opportunity to showcase an organization to different audiences and other professionals in attendance. Before deciding to attend and recruit at a job fair, an organization should make sure it is an appropriate job fair for their hiring needs. For example, it would not make sense for a company to attend a college job fair if the hiring needs were for professionals with five years of management experience. Similarly, the costs, time, and effort needed to prepare for a job fair should be taken into consideration. There needs to be a good return on this recruiting method for the organization. In other words, a significant amount of potential job applicants should be identified as a result of the job fair.

Word of mouth is a tried-and-true method of recruitment. Basically, it means that current employees, or those familiar with the hiring needs of an organization, talk with their friends, their associates, and people in their network about job openings. This type of advertising is usually a reliable supplement to more traditional recruiting methods and can also be quite effective and cost-efficient. Word of mouth is particularly useful with employers of choice—usually large, well-known brands or multinational companies—because they are frequently approached by job seekers for employment in their company. These jobs are viewed as coveted positions. Also, very small companies or businesses that are the main employer in a given location can benefit by communicating to as many people as possible that there are open positions in their organization.

Online recruitment advertising is a method used by organizations to attract potential job candidates via various forms of web-based media outlets. It is available in many different formats and for different strategic hiring objectives. However, it is not a one-size-fits-all recruitment method because the choice depends on an organization's desired audience, timing, related costs, and marketing plan. The following is an overview of several formats for recruitment advertising:
- **Job boards**—These are websites used by employers to advertise their job openings and where job seekers search for open positions. There are many job boards for employment, such as Indeed and Glassdoor. Deciding upon which job board(s) to use to advertise the job openings depends on the position, size of potential audience, cost of advertising, and possibly integration with an organization's applicant tracking system. Additionally, job boards are considered to be user-friendly, making it easy for a candidate to apply.
- **Niche job sites**—These sites specialize in posting jobs specific to a certain industry or position, or for a specified job seeker. These could be sponsored by clubs; professional organizations; or really any grouping, such as groups of accountants, medical assistants, or those who have virtual employment.
- **Social networks**—Most social networks such as Facebook and LinkedIn provide job-posting capabilities. Also, technologies like artificial intelligence and machine learning used by these networks have the potential to display targeted job ads for a specific audience.

Discuss the role of internal promotions, transfers, and former employees as a method for recruitment.

Summarize the methods and advantages of resume mining.

Define staffing agencies and typical services provided.

Describe a recruitment firm and its core functions.

Discuss the difference between a structured and unstructured interview.

Explain the main characteristics of a behavioral interview.

Resume mining can be a beneficial tool to use when sourcing candidates. Resume mining involves using search terms to scour the resume database on a job board (such as Indeed or ZipRecruiter) or applicant tracking system (ATS) a way to identify candidates who have qualifications that match an open position.

- The searchable resumes in a job board belong to people who have applied for a job via the site, or who have uploaded their resume in hopes of being discovered and contacted by employers looking to hire people with their credentials.
- The resumes in a company's ATS belong to people who have applied to work with the company.

Resume mining makes it possible to use technology to quickly identify applicants in the pool who have required skills or experience. It reduces the time it would take for a human to review resumes in search of specific qualifications. However, it's important to avoid using search terms that are too specific or too limited. Without using a variety of descriptive search terms, it would be easy to overlook the resumes of some strong candidates.

A **recruitment firm** is an external vendor that supplements an organization's internal recruiting effort, primarily helping an organization hire full-time, permanent employees. A recruiting firm usually has a network of potential candidates with whom they have fostered a relationship. Other times, a recruitment firm may be utilized for a specialized role that internal recruiters may not have experience hiring. This type of specialized recruiting is sometimes referred to as "niche recruiting." Similarly, a recruitment firm could also specialize in executive recruiting through their network of pre-identified, qualified candidates; these firms are sometimes called "headhunters." In many cases, regardless of the position, the recruiter will handle the initial screenings by sifting through resumes and conducting phone screenings and first interviews so that they can present qualified candidates to the organization. Some organizations—especially startups, smaller companies, and those with infrequent staffing needs—may not have an internal recruiter and may find it more efficient to use a recruitment firm.

Recruitment firms can be an advantageous external partner to an organization, but there are a few drawbacks. For example, they are not fully immersed in an organization's culture, and thus are not always able to represent the organization completely. They also may not be totally aware of the exact skills an organization is seeking in a candidate, and may be a bit slower to understand small nuances to changing candidate requirements. Overall, external recruitment firms that are measurably recruiting good hires are beneficial to partner with, as long as there is open communication.

A **behavioral interview** is a common interview technique designed to assess how an interviewee reacted to past job-related situations. The rationale is that future behavior can be predicted based on past behavior, especially behavior in the workplace. In a behavioral interview, the interviewer will not ask about certain desired skills; instead, they will ask the interviewee to speak about an occasion or circumstance where they displayed knowledge of a certain skill. An interviewer is trying to assess how an applicant behaved in the past versus how they will behave in the future. Common questions in a behavioral interview include, "Tell me about a time when you had to handle a difficult situation with a coworker," or "Can you think of an occasion when you had a hard deadline for a project and were constantly interrupted with unrelated matters?" The interviewer will often ask follow-up questions looking for details—asking specifically what was said or felt, or why the applicant said something or reacted the way they did. Throughout the interview, the interviewer is assessing the applicant's behavioral responses to workplace scenarios.

The best way for an interviewee to prepare for this type of interview is to try and remember stories they feel may be related to the job description. A useful method to accomplish this for the interviewee is the STAR technique: recall a **specific** situation, identify the **tasks** needed to be accomplished, the **actions** taken, and the end **result**.

Internal recruiting, defined as identifying and selecting a candidate within an organization, is sometimes used when it is not optimal or possible to find the desired requirements from external candidates. There may be open positions that require certain knowledge or skills that can be easily obtained from an individual already within an organization. Organizations may prefer internal hires for many reasons, including a motivational incentive for employees to work harder, an increase in company morale, or knowledge of an employee's pre-existing skill set and past performance evaluations. Internal hiring is an efficient recruiting methodology for large and small organizations across a wide variety of industries. One of the common methods for internal recruiting is **promotions,** whereby an individual is selected for a hierarchically higher position that usually includes an increase in compensation and responsibilities. A promotion is sometimes seen as a reward for previously displaying talent in a particular area.

Similar to a promotion, a **transfer** involves moving an employee from one job to another job that is comparable in some way. A transfer can be referred to as a lateral movement within an organization because it is a shift that is usually without substantial changes in responsibilities or compensation. A transfer may occur for a variety of reasons: it gives an employee a wider experience within the organization, it may improve any conflicts that arise in the current situation, or a slight change in position may relieve employee boredom.

A different method for internal recruiting is through **former employees**, those who left the organization on good terms for any number of different reasons. Former employees understand the company, and the organization is familiar with the former employees. This method could also reduce cost per hire.

A **staffing agency** is an external vendor that offers employees for an organization to hire, usually for temporary assignments. Staffing agencies can be industry-focused, specialized, or broader-based across industries and specialties. The most important distinction is that the staffing agency hires the worker. Therefore, the agency is the employer of record, not the organization. Hence, it is the staffing agency and not the organization that payrolls the worker and offers benefits. Typically, staffing agencies work with candidates that might be considered more entry- to mid-level management. Frequently, staffing agencies are utilized during a company's busiest season, during special projects, or possibly to replace someone on leave. Additionally, most staffing agencies interview, test, and prepare workers for placement instead of the organization.

A **structured interview** is when the interviewer has a predetermined set of questions that are asked of each interviewee, so that their responses can be fairly compared to one another. An **unstructured interview** is when the interviewer may have a few questions beforehand, but the majority of the interview is more spontaneous or unplanned. Basically, each interviewee may be asked different questions depending on the direction of the question and follow-up questions.

A structured interview is measurable in the sense that the questions are the same and the responses could be judged against one another with a quantitative component. An unstructured interview is more qualitative in that the information gathered is not equally comparable, but more insight into the applicant may be obtained. A structured interview is frequently used when there is a large candidate pool that needs to be compared to one another in order to judge who may be a better fit. An unstructured interview might be more useful when there are fewer candidates with qualifications that are almost identical, but the hiring manager needs to have a better feel for their thoughts and personality.

Summarize the objectives of a situational interview.

Describe what occurs during a panel interview.

Summarize some of the elements of a group interview.

Explain the purpose of a stress interview and how one is undertaken.

Explain the importance of skills assessments and how they are used.

Describe which aspects of the hiring and recruiting process should be free from bias.

A **panel interview** is when a group of people interview a prospective job candidate at the same time. The panel of interviewers are typically brought together in order to get different perspectives about whether or not a candidate is a good fit for a position. Panel members tend to be those who will interact with the hired individual and have a good understanding of the organization and its culture. However, an effective panel interview should have a diverse assortment of personalities and viewpoints to accurately assess candidates. Everyone on the panel should also be allowed to freely offer their honest opinion. The goal of a panel interview is for the panelists to offer their insights and collectively reduce the risk in hiring a candidate that will not be a good fit. Usually, the hiring manager leads the panel, but individuals on the panel often have opening questions, and possibly follow-up questions that can be asked by anyone on the panel. Typically, this type of interview is longer than a traditional interview—about 90 minutes to 2 hours. Panel interviews can be conducted in many industries and for a variety of positions, but are most often used in senior executive positions, public-sector government organizations or agencies, academic institutions, and large not-for-profit organizations.

During a **situational interview**, the interviewee is usually provided a scenario and then asked how he or she would respond. The objective of a situational interview is for the interviewer to gauge the interviewee's reaction to any number of conditions, including their behavior and how a problem is solved. These responses are then used to evaluate how the interviewee would perform when faced with similar situations on the job. It could be said that behavioral interviews look at the past and situational interviews look at the future. The questions in a situational interview are frequently hypothetical, such as, "If you knew your boss was making a wrong decision, how would you handle it?" or "What would you do in the following situation?" The questions are usually related to actual problems encountered in the workplace. The interviewer is interested in hearing if the interviewee has the basic knowledge to answer the question and solve the problem, exhibiting expertise in their profession or job. The interviewer may also listen to his or her ability to quickly assess the situation, and to the logic behind decisions.

A **stress interview** creates a scenario whereby the interviewee is placed under some form of psychological (not physical) pressure and then evaluated on how well the individual operates under stress. Most other types of interviews try to put the interviewee at ease and garner information by engaging in a respectful communication exchange. Stress interviews are usually only used by certain industries and for specific positions that will encounter a tremendous amount of stress on the job. For example, stress interviews are sometimes used by law enforcement, sales agencies, and airlines. These are positions that may encounter conflict and rudeness daily.

Stress interviews can be conducted any number of ways, but generally the interviewer could use words to deliberately intimidate the interviewee, make the interviewee wait a long period of time, interrupt frequently, ask the same questions multiple times, act aggressively, walk around while asking questions, raise their voice, speak very softly, etc. The goal for the interviewer is to evaluate how calm the interviewee remains or if the individual buckles under the pressure. It is extremely important to note that stress interviews are controversial and reserved only for special positions. Legal counsel should be consulted before designing and implementing a stress interview.

A **group interview** consists of one or more interviewers who interview several interviewees at the same time. Group interview situations are more likely to occur in the hospitality industry, meaning hotel employment, rental agents, food service, and retail. Interviewing many people at once is time-efficient. Additionally, group interviews give the interviewer an opportunity to see and hear how well the interviewees interact with one another and behave under stress. Social interaction and stress under pressure are the two key characteristics of those who work in the industries noted above. Typically, interviewees are informed of the group interview format ahead of time so they are not surprised. The person(s) doing the interview will usually prepare questions ahead of time, and also be able to pivot and change direction if follow-up or clarification is needed. Group interviews usually begin with the interviewer(s) making the candidates comfortable and asking each one to say a little about himself or herself. Ground rules for courtesy and respect are outlined, and then the interviewer(s) begin asking questions.

Every aspect of the recruiting and hiring process should be free from bias. This means that everyone involved in the process should take care to avoid prejudging applicants based on perceptions they may have regarding traits, characteristics, or individual differences.
Bias can be conscious or unconscious, so it's important to be aware of some of the ways that bias may find its way into the hiring process.

Skills assessments can be an important part of the applicant screening process. For example, a job may require creating or troubleshooting spreadsheets using advanced functions like pivot tables or "if" statements. However, the fact that an applicant's resume lists Excel as a skill doesn't necessarily mean that they have the level of ability required for the position. Instead of just asking if they know how to work with pivot tables or "if" statements, a hiring manager could have them complete a skills assessment that requires them to apply their expertise. This is a more objective way of verifying their skill level.

The job description is a great tool for identifying what kinds of skills assessments could be beneficial in the hiring process. Hiring managers can use the list of essential job functions to make a list of skills that candidates must have, then decide the best way to determine if the candidate's abilities meet the requirements. This may involve working with management to create skills assessments specific to certain jobs or purchasing pre-employment assessments from a testing vendor.

Pre-employment skill assessment platforms like eSkill and TestGorilla offer many skill-specific tests, including skills with computer applications, quantitative skills, verbal skills, and customer service. Their tests can be used as is or customized based on job requirements. Skills assessments used in the hiring process must be free from bias and administered in a nondiscriminatory way.

Define the different types of biases that may occur during the hiring and recruiting process.

Summarize how reference checks work and their importance.

Define the information that should be included in an offer letter.

Describe a counteroffer and the various proposals it may include.

Explain the various aspects of an employment contract and when they are used.

Summarize some cautionary measures employers can take when designing drug testing programs.

Before offering a job to a candidate, it's a good idea to check the individual's references. This generally involves contacting an individual's previous employers to verify the information on their application and to ask about their work habits and behavior. It may also involve contacting personal or professional references provided by the candidate.

- Companies often have policies that restrict subjective references, so previous employers usually only provide fact-based information such as verifying dates of employment, job title, compensation, and whether the individual is eligible for rehire.
- Personal or other professional references may provide more subjective information, such as information about a candidate's character, work ethic, or communication style.

Reference checks may be conducted by phone, mail, or email. An employer may contact references directly or use the services of a background screening company.

- **Stereotyping**—Making assumptions based on generalizations, such as assuming that someone who has been a manager won't want a non-supervisory job, or assuming that a female applicant won't want a job that requires extensive travel.
- **Halo effect**—Allowing something perceived as positive to overshadow other information, such as assuming that an applicant who attended a prestigious college must be an ideal candidate even if they don't have much (or any) experience.
- **Horns effect**—Allowing something perceived as negative to overshadow positive characteristics, such as dismissing a candidate from being considered because they were flustered at the beginning of an interview even though they have all required skills and are otherwise a good fit.
- **Confirmation bias**—Making up your mind about a candidate and then only paying attention to information that reinforces what you already believe (for example, deciding that a candidate has poor attention to detail and then looking for slip-ups that reinforce that belief while disregarding evidence to the contrary).
- **Contrast bias**—Comparing a candidate to a particular individual—such as the person who is leaving the job or a preferred candidate who turned down the position—instead of to the essential job functions and other job requirements.
- **Gender bias**—Assuming that a job is more suited to a person of a particular gender, such as presuming that men lack the listening skills to work in a call center, or that women aren't strong enough for production work.
- **Similar-to-me bias**—Presuming that candidates who share characteristics in common with the interviewer are best-suited for the job, such as showing preference to a candidate who is from the interviewer's hometown or attended the same college.

If a candidate declines an initial offer, the company may wish to make a counteroffer based on the reasons the candidate gave for declining. For example, a counteroffer may include:

- Higher rate of pay
- Sign-on bonus
- Retention bonus
- More paid time off (PTO)
- Revised or flexible schedule
- Other inducements

Counteroffers should be made in writing and include the same type of information as an initial job offer.

It is best practice for job offers to be made in writing, in the form of an offer letter. An offer letter should include:

- Job title
- Salary or hourly rate of pay
- Job classification (exempt or nonexempt)
- Expected start date
- Work location
- Contingencies (such as background check, drug test, fit-for-duty physical)
- Usual work schedule or shift
- Benefits overview
- Relocation package (if applicable)
- Contact information for questions
- Deadline to accept or decline
- How to accept or decline

Many employers utilize drug testing to screen applicants and, in some cases, current employees. Generally speaking, employers can legally require applicants to pass a **drug test** as a condition of employment or adopt programs that test active employees as long as the programs are not discriminatory. Due to the controversial nature of drug testing, employers must be meticulously cautious when designing these programs to ensure practices will be upheld if brought to court. In addition, employers should make sure their drug testing program and related policies are in compliance with all state and local laws. For example, employers in some states can document that they have a zero-tolerance policy for drug usage, such as repercussions including employee termination, while employers in other states need to promote assistance programs for drug use. It is important to remember that the drug test results received from the testing company are confidential and should be filed and secured separately from the hired employee's personnel file. *Wilkinson v. Times Mirror Corporation* established the following elements for testing programs:

- Samples are collected at a medical facility by persons unrelated to the employer.
- Applicants are unobserved by others when they furnish samples.
- Results are kept confidential.
- The medical lab only notifies employers of whether the applicant passed or failed.
- Applicants are notified by the medical lab of the portion they failed—some instances will provide applicants an opportunity to present medical documentation prior to the employer receiving results.
- There is a defined method for applicants to question or challenge test results.
- Applicants must be eligible to reapply after a reasonable time.

When a company offers a job to a candidate and the candidate accepts, the job offer itself becomes a contract. This is true whether the offer is made verbally or in writing. It's best for offers to be made and accepted in writing so there is no question regarding the terms and conditions.

In some cases, an employer may also have a new hire sign an employment contract, also referred to as an employment agreement. This type of document has more detail than the offer letter and may include specific performance requirements such as sales quotas, revenue or profitability targets, or other performance metrics, along with the consequences if specified benchmarks are not achieved. An employment contract may also include a noncompete agreement, confidentiality requirements, or ownership of intellectual property.

Formal employment contracts are not required in the United States, but they are fairly common for executive-level positions and sales jobs, as well as other positions with specific production or performance requirements. Some employers use employment contracts for most or all positions. A company should consult with legal counsel to draw up employment contracts.

List some employer considerations regarding pre-employment background checks.

Explain when a post-offer medical exam is needed and the related procedures.

Describe the process of issuing company-mandated documents to new employees.

Explain how an employee handbook should be distributed.

Describe the difference between an employee handbook and various formal agreements.

Summarize the information included in benefits paperwork and how it is distributed.

A post-offer medical exam is usually requested by an employer to evaluate if the selected person can safely perform the essential functions of the job in such a manner as to not risk injury to themselves or anyone else. The medical exam findings can also help determine if the individual will need accommodations in order to safely perform the job. The decision to institute a medical exam is based on detailed job requirements that clearly document which positions specifically require a medical exam. An employer usually has a written policy about which applicants need exams, procedures, and advance notification to the candidate of this requirement.

Employer planning is necessary to set up a cost-effective medical examination program with a third-party doctor performing the medical exam. The doctor must be completely familiar with the job requirements and necessary good health needed to perform those duties. The doctor's summary report back to the employer is only supposed to contain information that will impact the individual's ability to perform the job, and nothing else, in order to maintain the examinee's privacy. It is important to remember that the file received from the doctor is confidential and should be filed and secured separately from the hired employee's personnel file.

A company should distribute an employee handbook or policy manual to new employees at the beginning of employee orientation so that new hires can become familiar with company policies and procedures right away.

The handbook can be printed, emailed, or posted to the company intranet in a manner that all employees can access. Employees should be provided with time to review each document and ask questions before signing an acknowledgement that will be stored in their personnel file.

New employees should be provided with benefits paperwork on the first day of orientation, including details about each plan. Depending on what the company offers, this may include information about the company's health insurance, retirement plan, life insurance, dental plan, vision coverage, cafeteria plan for health and dependent care expenses, and available supplemental group benefits.

Benefits paperwork may be distributed in print or digital form. It should include:
- Plan details
- Cost
- Eligibility
- Enrollment forms

New employees should be given a few days to review the information so they can make an informed decision on which benefits they want. They should also be informed of the company's open enrollment date, so they'll know how long they'll have to wait to opt in on any benefits that they decline at this time. The company should collect their benefits enrollment paperwork, along with documentation that specifies any benefits they are declining.

Many employers will conduct pre-employment background checks on candidates to ensure that employees have sound judgment and are unlikely to engage in improper conduct and/or do not have a criminal record. HR departments often order credit checks or criminal record searches through online service providers and then review results. The Fair Credit Reporting Act, like many legal regulations, requires not only that employers notify applicants that they administer background checks, but also that applicants must sign a written release consenting that the employer may receive their personal information. Furthermore, when implementing a pre-employment background check, employers must consider if doing so may be discriminatory, and therefore must validate the business necessity.

Many states have joined the Ban the Box movement, which prohibits employers from asking about an applicant's criminal history at the time of application. If an offense is found, employers are urged to consider the severity of the offense, the amount of time elapsed since the offense, and whether the offense is related to the nature of the job. Applicants must also have the opportunity to contest or explain adverse results before officially being turned down for employment. The prospective employer must furnish a copy of the report to the applicant. The Federal Trade Commission advises employers to give the applicant five days to respond before sending them an official letter of rejection.

A company should distribute company-mandated documents to new hires on their first day of employment. Employees should be required to sign off indicating that they have received, read, and understood each document.

An employee handbook isn't a contract and doesn't extend to former employees. Any policy that needs to extend beyond an individual's employment and/or be legally binding should be presented to employees as a formal agreement that they're required to sign, separate from the employee handbook or policy manual.

A nondisclosure agreement (NDA) is an example of a document that companies often require employees to sign separate from the handbook or policy manual. The purpose of an NDA is to protect the confidentiality of important company information, such as client lists, marketing strategies, and product formulations. This type of document is particularly important for employees with access to proprietary information.

Other documents that employers often require employees to sign as standalone agreements may include, but are not limited to, a noncompete agreement, privacy policy, anti-harassment policy, or code of ethics. Signed agreements should be kept in each employee's personnel file.

Explain the difference between onboarding and orientation.

Describe the basics of the onboarding process.

Detail some common topics covered during onboarding.

Summarize the various aspects of an employee orientation.

Discuss why technology-based tools are needed to compile data.

Explain the purpose of an applicant tracking system.

Visit *mometrix.com/academy* for a related video.
Enter video code: 532324

Onboarding, sometimes called organizational socialization, is a strategically choreographed process that enables a new employee to holistically understand an organization, its culture, and how the individual fits into the business. Onboarding varies depending on the organization and the position. There is not one particular correct format because it is dependent on many factors. However, the overall goal is to assist the employee with being a productive contributor. The onboarding process can be a few months to a couple years, although one year is more common.

The terms "onboarding" and "orientation" are sometimes used interchangeably, but there is a difference. **Onboarding** is the overall strategic process of acclimating a new hire into the business and its culture. This process can last anywhere from a month to a couple years. Meanwhile, **orientation** is a part of the onboarding process designed to introduce new employees to their specific job, including colleagues and others they may interact with on the job. Orientations are one-time events, but depending on the organization and the job, they can last anywhere from an hour to a few days. During an orientation, the new hire will be instructed about their specific job and the tools, methodologies, interactions, and instructions needed to perform the job. An orientation is critical in the onboarding process because it helps the new hire understand how their position contributes to overall organizational goals.

Orientation is the first step in the onboarding process and the beginning of the employer-employee relationship. Orientation tends to be more administrative in nature, as it is usually a series of tasks that need to be completed before an employee can proceed into their specific role. For example, it may include a tour of the work facilities, I-9 verification, benefit selection, payroll forms, and processing information. Orientation also covers company policies and where to go for various types of information. An overview of the organization and introductions may also take place. Orientation is a two-way process, in that an employee's questions and concerns are discussed and answered. The goal of orientation is not only to get the new employee paperwork processed logistics handled, and introductions made, but to help the new employee feel welcome and quickly transition into being a productive employee.

Typically, the following is covered during the onboarding process, though not necessarily in this order, and delivery methods could include virtual, in-person classroom, self-directed learning, one-on-one instruction, and meet-and-greets:

- An overview of **policies and benefits**—This may include paperwork that needs to be completed, such as benefit selection, payroll, proof of citizenship, emergency contact information, and an instructional overview of company policies and procedures, including the employee handbook and the organization's diversity policy. This portion of onboarding could also be called "orientation."
- Understanding how the **role fits into the organization**—This includes information about an employee's job expectations and related interactions with other areas of the organization.
- Customized **role-specific training**—Training can be conducted with the employee's supervisor or any other person knowledgeable about the position. Many organizations have a continuous learning environment to maintain a competitive advantage, making it an ongoing process.
- Organizational **culture training**—This can be a formal or more casual process whereby an employee learns company values and engages in activities related to vision and mission, such as team-building events, dinners, and classroom trainings.
- **Facilitated social connections**—This could be a simple meet-and-greet facilitated by the employee's manager, a formal "buddy system" whereby another more tenured employee is assigned to help facilitate social connections, or many other scenarios.

An **applicant tracking system** (ATS) is a computer database used by employers to automate and manage all or some aspects of the job application and hiring process. Other names used for ATS programs include talent acquisition software, recruitment software, hiring database, or hiring platform. The primary purpose of an ATS is to efficiently manage information in the job application process. An ATS captures everything an applicant submits for a job posting, including name, resume, education, experience, contact information, and cover letter. In response, the ATS can be programmed by a recruiter to filter resumes for keywords or experiences, give online tests, schedule interviews, mail rejection letters (if applicable), and much more. An ATS allows multiple people to view job candidate information, including interview notes and evaluations. After a candidate is selected, the information obtained in the ATS can often be seamlessly transitioned to other software, such as a payroll system. An ATS creates efficiencies that allow an employer to optimize the hiring process.

HR utilizes large volumes of data about the organization and the people it employs for the purpose of recruitment, performance management and evaluations, payroll, equal employment opportunity (EEO), etc. Tools to compile data make organizational functions more efficient and productive. Some tools are unique to HR management, such as a human resource information system (HRIS), and others are more commonplace, like Microsoft Office with Excel, Word, and PowerPoint. HR specifically compiles data to include types of employees, employee specifics, compensation, training, open jobs, etc. This type of data is vital to HR for many reasons, such as budgeting, succession planning, salary surveys and reviews, ensuring EEO compliance, and applicant presentations. It is important to remember that different tools or software are used for different purposes. Therefore, the key is to understand available HR tools and software and use those that best suit the functions needed for a specific project. Frequently, it is necessary to filter and download data from one source or tool and bring it into another to optimize data manipulation or present information. An example of this would be using data from an HRIS to complete an Excel file.

Explain how an applicant tracking system (ATS) can be utilized for applicant flow data reporting.

Describe some advantages that an ATS gives an employer in hiring.

Describe some advantages that an ATS gives an employer in reporting and onboarding.

Discuss some safeguards an employer should be aware of when using an applicant tracking system (ATS).

Explain the advantages and disadvantages of technology systems that HR professionals utilize.

Describe a spreadsheet and its key functions.

There are many specific benefits an employer can derive from utilizing an ATS:

- **Job posting**—Employers can post job requisitions across multiple third-party job boards as well as in a company job posting.
- **Easier application process for candidates**—Job candidates can more expediently apply for jobs via an ATS, allowing an employer to be seen as more favorable.
- **More efficient resume filtering**—Due to specialized keyword searches across resumes, recruiters can eliminate resumes more quickly.
- **Everything is in one spot**—Manage everything about a job applicant in one place, with no need for spreadsheets or computer folders.
- **Increases overall administrative efficiency**—More efficiently complete administrative tasks associated with recruiting and hiring job candidates, including resume filtering, phone screenings, evaluations, interview scheduling, and tests.

Applicant flow tracking is required by the Equal Employment Opportunity Commission (EEOC) and necessary for any employer to complete if they have a federal contract. The information should detail the gender and race of every applicant that applies for an open position. The objective is to analyze source data and identify the selection rate among groupings by race and gender for a position to ensure that a fair grouping of people is being sourced for the open job. Organizations with a federal contract are supposed to make a reasonable effort to collect and maintain this information. Typically, this information is voluntarily self-reported by the job candidate or casually observed by an HR representative in an interview situation.

An ATS assists in the recordkeeping of this information as well as the ability to generate reports needed to analyze the data. It is extremely important to note this information cannot be used in hiring decisions. During the application process, the job applicant is also made aware, in writing, that the hiring decision will not be based on self-reported EEOC-related personal information. In fact, HR is to secure that information, either electronically or in paper format, and keep it separate from the employee's application. An ATS makes collecting and reporting this type of data more accurate and efficient.

Overall, an ATS makes the recruitment process more efficient, but there are some limitations an employer should consider and address. Frequently an ATS is used to filter out resumes if the candidate does not have a certain skill or experience. This filter is based on a pattern of keywords. If applicants have the desired skill or experience, and they use synonyms or words not close enough to the keyword filters, then they might be eliminated from consideration. Furthermore, an ATS sometimes has character-restricted fields, meaning that a candidate might be qualified, but the character restriction did not allow them to provide enough information. Occasionally, an ATS might scan a resume incorrectly; this could occur if there is something in the resume that the system is not programmed to recognize. Usually, an ATS can be modified, and recruiters usually make an effort to ensure that qualified candidates do not slip through the cracks.

There are many specific benefits an employer can derive from utilizing an ATS:

- **Captures and tracks job applicant data for reporting**—Efficiently and accurately capture job applicant information that may need to be tracked and reported to comply with Equal Employment Opportunity (EEO) and Office of Federal Contract Compliance Programs (OFCCP) regulations. Allows an employer to analyze the database of applicants for specific EEO categories and job classifications. Additionally, an employer can use the database for recruiting analytics.
- **Assists in the onboarding process**—An ATS streamlines the onboarding of a selected job candidate, as the information captured in the ATS can usually be transferred to other systems an employer might utilize, such as payroll or information technology. This may also eliminate a significant amount of paperwork.

A **spreadsheet** is a computer application used to store, analyze, and organize data in a tabular format of horizontal rows and vertical columns. Data, both numeric and text, is entered into cells that can be used to calculate and display information. For example, a spreadsheet could contain information such as employee names, job titles, locations, and compensation, which could be used to calculate compensation information by title or location. This information can also be referred to as a database. One of the most popular spreadsheet programs is Microsoft Excel. The following are some key functions performed in Excel for HR analysis:

- Query—A request for data that filters and formats information from a spreadsheet or database.
- Sorting—The process of arranging data in a specific order, such as alphabetical or lowest to highest.
- Filter—A condition that qualifies data to be revealed or hidden, such as showing data from a certain location or department.
- Vlookup—a function that returns a specific piece of information by looking up a supplied entry name and finding data in a specified column.
- Pivot table—Permits data to be summarized using interactive fields and filter buttons. Enables easy retrieval of specific data from a large amount of data.

A **human resource information system** (HRIS) enables employees to have greater and more expedient access to their personal HR-related data. Some advanced HRIS programs allow employees to immediately request time off, change their mailing address, adjust 401(k) contributions, etc. In this respect, HR technology has automated very labor-intensive paperwork, thereby creating more organizational efficiencies and possibly enabling HR professionals to expand into more strategic roles.

An **applicant tracking system** (ATS) automates the application process from the beginning through the hiring of an employee. This has many benefits for realizing efficiencies, but could also overwhelm recruiters with unqualified candidates they must weed through.

An HR **knowledge management system** (KMS) is a central repository for HR information that can be quickly accessed by employees, usually considered a 24/7 self-service portal. Frequently, it may provide access to onboarding information, benefit selection and policy information, requests for time off and historical attendance information, general HR policy information, etc. The main benefits of a KMS include the increased ability for an employee to quickly access information, that the information can be updated easily and thus reduce misinformation, and that it reduces the administrative workload for HR. However, the system needs to be maintained, and permissions must be managed so that employees have access only to information that is pertinent to them.

Integration of technology tools—HR now has many technological tools to manage employees. Access to too much data, and sometimes irrelevant data, can be a consideration in effective data usage. Also, the integration of various technology platforms can be challenging.

Summarize some of the statistical tools used in HR to compile data.

Explain return on investment.

Explain return on equity.

Explain cost per hire.

Explain how to calculate cost per hire.

Define the equation used to determine cost per hire and how to calculate it.

Return on investment (ROI) is a ratio or percentage comparing the gains of an investment versus its initial price. In other words, ROI measures the return of an investment relative to the cost. The formula is:

$$\text{ROI} = \frac{\text{Value investment} - \text{Cost investment}}{\text{Cost investment}}$$

For example:

- A company invests in an applicant tracking system (ATS) that costs $15,000.
- The company has been paying a staffing agency $25,000 per year to screen entry-level applications. (This can be calculated manually from invoices, or more simply by using the company's tech-based accounting platform to pull a report.)
- The ATS allows the company to bring entry-level candidate screening in-house without incurring additional related expenses.

To calculate ROI, first determine the gain, which, in this case, is the amount of money the company saves because of investing in an ATS. The company eliminated a $25,000 staffing agency expense by spending $15,000 on an ATS, so the gain is $10,000. ROI is the gain realized by the investment, divided by the cost of the investment:

$$\text{ROI} = \frac{\$25,000 - \$15,000}{\$15,000} = \frac{\$10,000}{\$15,000} = 0.67, \text{ or } 67\%$$

The example above shows the manual calculation, but a company can set up an ROI formula template using spreadsheet software. With that in place, calculating ROI would be as simple as plugging in data pulled from the IT system and the actual expenditure.

Cost per hire is an HR recruitment metric that measures the total money invested to hire someone divided by the number of hires in a given time period. Internal costs might include employee referral awards, recruiter salaries, or cost of internal recruiting systems. External costs might include advertising, events, job fairs, background checks, or assessments.

The formula is:

$$\text{Cost per hire} = \frac{\text{Total internal \& external recruiting costs}}{\text{Total number of hires in given time period}}$$

This is a strategic metric used to assess the efficiency and effectiveness in an organization's recruiting process, and is frequently benchmarked against similar organizations and industry peers.

If a company's total recruitment costs for a year are $150,000 and the firm hired 50 employees that year, the cost-per-hire calculation would be $\frac{\$150,000}{50} = \$3,000$. That means the company has a cost per hire of $3,000.

This can be calculated manually, but setting up a template in a spreadsheet application would make this calculation as easy as plugging in data accessed via the company's technology systems.

An HRIS may even automatically calculate cost per hire on an ongoing basis. This is very beneficial, as having access to this metric makes it easy to stay aware of cost per hire and the impact of adjustments to recruiting expenditures in real time.

Statistics usage in HR is a data-driven approach to managing people and other variables in an organization. Statistics can help people understand a situation, can forecast future possibilities based on previously obtained data, and can sometimes help an organization mitigate risk. For example, statistics might help an organization better gauge when people will leave, discover possible bias in the hiring process, and help guide benefit decisions. There are many tools and software applications available to organizations for statistical analysis. The following are some commonly used HR statistical tools:

- R—A programming language that is a powerful statistical tool for data analysis and visualization, designed to manipulate enormous datasets.
- Python—Similar to R, offers fewer visualization and statistical analysis features, but is easier to learn.
- Power BI (business intelligence)—Statistical software that can aggregate large amounts of data as well as perform analysis and offer visualization benefits. Useful when multiple data sources need to be combined.
- Tableau platform—Similar to Power BI, good for aggregation of data and considered to be outstanding at visualization.
- Excel—The most basic statistical software for smaller sets of data and the easiest-to-use statistical package.

Return on equity (ROE) is a ratio or percentage measuring the earnings of the organization during a period of time as compared to the amount of money invested in shareholder equity. ROE reveals whether an organization is efficiently using investments to make profits by measuring the organization's rate of return on shareholder equity. In other words, it signals to shareholders whether their investment is being used wisely.

For example, suppose Company B has $1 million in net income and $10 million in shareholder equity. Dividing net income by shareholder equity reveals the ROE: $\frac{\$1 \text{ million}}{\$10 \text{ million}} = 10\%$. This is a 10% return on the shareholders' investment. Sometimes a company will compare their ROE with similar competitors in the field. The basic formula for ROE is:

$$\text{ROE} = \frac{\text{Net income}}{\text{Shareholder equity}}$$

Cost per hire is usually calculated annually but can also be considered on a quarterly basis. For example, a company that has a lot of seasonal college recruiting expenses may want to look at cost per hire for that specific timeframe separate from the rest of the year.

The first step in calculating cost per hire is to determine total recruitment costs for the designated time period. Total recruiting costs may include (but are not limited to):

- Recruiter salaries
- Compensation for others involved in recruiting, selection, and onboarding
- Cost of operating the careers page on the company website
- Applicant tracking system costs
- Candidate assessments, including skill testing and/or behavioral assessments
- Screening fees, such as background checks, drug tests, or fit-for-duty physical exams
- Other expenses related to recruiting and onboarding new hires

Coding recruitment-based expenses as such in the company's information technology system or accounting platform can be helpful. This makes it possible to quickly and easily pull a report from the information technology system that shows recruitment-related expenses in a defined period before a solution was implemented, and for the same length of time after the solution was implemented. Meanwhile, the HR information system (HRIS) makes it easy to quickly determine the total number of employees hired during those timeframes. This information can then be used to calculate cost per hire for those time periods.

Describe what time to fill is and how to calculate it.

Summarize and apply selection ratios.

Define turnover and turnover statistics.

Summarize new hires and the onboarding process.

Define "internal transfers" and "rehires."

Summarize how to set expectations with new hires and the importance of this process.

Selection ratio is used in the HR recruiting process to assess and evaluate sourcing for job positions. It is a ratio obtained by taking the number of candidates that the business desires to hire and dividing it by the total number of candidates for the open jobs. A low ratio means the organization can be more selective, while a high ratio indicates the organization need not be as selective. The formula for selection ratio is:

$$\text{Selection ratio} = \frac{\text{Number of hired candidates}}{\text{Total number of candidates}}$$

Selection ratios can be applied in many ways. For example, they can be used to evaluate applicant acceptance of offers; divide the number of offers accepted by those that were extended. Additionally, the percentage of minority applicants can be determined; take the number of minority applicants divided by the total number of applicants for that same position in the same time period.

New hires are employees recently added to an organization or team. They can be early in their career and just starting out, college graduates who are entering the workforce, or experienced hires who are switching roles or companies. New employees are expected to represent the organization in a responsible way in and out of work, partner collaboratively with stakeholders to achieve business results, and work with honesty and integrity. New hire expectations are frequently outlined in employee handbooks, which often include code of conduct policies that outline expectations for conduct and behavior.

Helping new hires establish themselves at work and understand the mission, goals, and ways of working can determine how quickly they adjust and start to add value. Onboarding is the process of socializing with new employees to share the knowledge, skills, behavior, and attitudes required to successfully function. Onboarding plans that provide visibility to leaders and decision makers and facilitate touchpoints with key partners help to provide structure and exposure at the right intervals for maximum impact. A successful onboarding plan should:

- Help new employees learn the company's mission, vision, values, and strategic goals.
- Help new employees understand performance expectations for their new role.
- Help new employees meet team members and internal stakeholders.
- Help new employees complete any compliance or regulatory requirements.
- Help new employees gain access to systems and tools necessary for the job.
- Help new employees complete personal tasks related to pay, benefits, and taxes.

A planned approach to setting expectations, building relationships, and acclimating new hires and employees is essential for a successful onboarding program.

Organizations must start early when setting expectations with new hires to increase their ability to add immediate value and to accelerate their performance. It is important to establish clear objectives to help employees understand the job duties and overall requirements for their role. They must understand how their responsibilities align to the larger organizational goals to increase their sense of belonging and connectedness. Management should:

- Explain to new hires what "good" looks like and share performance expectations that address how and why work gets done.
- Spend time reviewing company goals, how resources are structured, how the organization makes money, and desired behaviors and expectations. This will ensure employees understand the professional standards around conduct in and out of work.
- Help new joiners build relationships and form the right networks, and equip them with tools to boost collaboration.

Knowing the needs of each new hire and notifying internal stakeholders will help accelerate the new hire's ability to hit the ground running. As employees become active and visible within an organization, they are positioned to start building relationships in a more meaningful way.

Time to fill is an indicator of how long it takes a company to staff open positions. It is the length of time between when a position becomes available and when a candidate accepts the job.

Time to fill for a specific job is calculated by subtracting the offer position vacancy date from the offer acceptance date. For example, if a company opens a job order on July 1 and a candidate accepts the position on July 25, then the time to fill for that specific job is 24 days ($25 - 1 = 24$).

A company usually discusses time to fill as an average for a certain type of position over a specific period of time, such as annually or quarterly.

An ATS or HRIS is likely to provide this metric in real time, but it can also be calculated manually. Calculating average time to fill requires two steps:

- Calculate the sum of time to fill for all job openings of a certain type during the defined period of time.
- Divide that number by the total number of people hired for that type of position during the timeframe.

Average time to fill can help hiring managers know approximately how long they should expect a position to be open before it can realistically be filled, so it's important to evaluate this data point continually.

Time to fill can also help identify hiring difficulties or evaluate recruitment effectiveness. When time to fill starts to increase, that's a good time to evaluate whether the company needs to adjust its recruiting strategy or to reconsider job-related factors such as compensation, job design, or flexibility.

Turnover refers to when an employee permanently leaves an organization. Turnover is typically captured as a rate or percentage on a monthly or yearly basis and is useful in predicting the number of new employees that must be hired to replace those that have permanently left the organization. More often, turnover statistics are analyzed on a monthly basis to also highlight at what point in the year employees tend to exit the organization. The formula to calculate monthly employee turnover is:

Monthly turnover rate

$$= \frac{\text{Number of separations during month}}{\text{Average number of employees during month}} \times 100$$

For example, if 30 employees leave the organization in the month of January, and there was an average of 200 employees in the month of January, then the turnover rate is 15%. Turnover statistics are more than just a number or percentage. This rate gives an organization a starting point to analyze why employees are leaving and take corrective actions, if needed, to maintain a healthy organization. Some of the reasons for turnover might include poor performance, better pay, personal reasons, or career advancement.

Not all new hires are "new" to an organization. **Internal transfers** are existing employees who move teams or business units and have unique onboarding needs. They often have experience with the company and don't need to complete the same administrative tasks as new hires but require assimilation to new projects, processes, and teams. **Rehires** are former employees who are hired again and rejoin an organization. These groups have unique needs to be considered when planning onboarding, such as bridging tenure, benefits, or other policies that may have been in place during their prior tenure. Understanding the different types of new hires—and their unique requirements—will help with the effectiveness of employee orientation programs.

Describe how team members and HR professionals can help new hires transition into a company.

Summarize onboarding programs and their importance.

Describe the importance of establishing a tailored learning strategy.

Summarize formal training programs.

Summarize informal training.

Define knowledge management and its importance.

Helping employees understand the goals, strategy, and structure of an organization helps them connect their individual contributions to the overall success of the company. Sharing information about leadership teams, department structures, and how they work together adds clarity and helps orient new employees in an organization. Employee training is a critical function of onboarding. Training requirements can vary by industry or role, and can be required before employees gain access to critical internal systems and documentation. Helping employees understand what they need to do, by when, and why, is important in helping them understand how work is performed. This training becomes a platform to introduce important policies and processes, as well as provide contact information for follow-up questions.

Robust onboarding programs account for all resources that perform work on behalf of a company, not just new hires or employees. This can include:

- Internal transfers
- Temporary workers (interns, co-ops)
- Contingent workers (contractors, consultants, freelancers)
- Rehires

HR professionals play an important role in planning and structuring onboarding programs that satisfy individual, team, and business needs. Investing in employees through salary, benefits, and training and development is often a company's biggest expense. Supporting employees during this critical transition can affect an employee's tenure, satisfaction, and productivity, which all impact company profitability.

New hires can reset where a team is in the group development cycle. Onboarding employees is often a team activity—work gets restructured, and existing team members are tasked to support a new team member either directly or indirectly. Team members can offer support formally, by acting as a resource and knowledge partner. Informally, they can help clarify information, provide useful history and background, and guide employees on where to find support and resources. Creating the right connections early—with peers, team members, leadership, and the broader organization—enhances feelings of belongingness and shortens the time it takes for an employee to start adding value. Opportunities such as mentoring programs and employee resource groups help to foster a sense of connection and belonging at work while providing exposure to more of the business. A successful transition into the company can increase feelings of connection to the team and the broader company mission. Relationships are key to helping employees acclimate and navigate a company's culture. HR leaders can support employees in building relationships within a department or on project teams. Below are some important ways HR can support relationship-building for new employees:

- Encourage organization announcements to introduce new employees.
- Structure relationship building with direct reports, line managers, and other stakeholders using onboarding calendars.
- Promote information relationship building using mentorship or buddy programs.
- Create onboarding templates to ensure a standardized experience for all new employees.
- Invite employees to connect with internal affinity groups or volunteer efforts.

HR professionals can help employees establish relationships that are essential for success. Developing onboarding plans and designing systems with the right one-on-one and team touchpoints can facilitate meaningful relationships and partnerships.

Formal training refers to the planned teaching of a particular skill or behavior. The objective of training is to facilitate the mastery of knowledge, skills, and abilities in job-related competency areas. At work, training is often presented in the form of dedicated events, which can be hosted in-person or online. Formal training can be instructor-led, by internal or external experts, and is often accompanied by physical or digital supporting material that participants can reference during or after the presentation. Formal training events offer flexibility in scope and are suitable for individuals, teams, or entire organizations.

Training and development is one of several critical functions within HR departments. The goal of training and development in the overall business context is to promote learning. Learning refers to the acquisition of the knowledge, skills, competence, and experience that result in lasting behavior change. A learning organization is one that promotes a culture of lifelong development, provides formal and informal learning opportunities, and enables employees to acquire job-related skills and experiences. Establishing an organizational learning strategy has many benefits:

- It provides a proven method of increasing the knowledge, skills, experience, and abilities of employees.
- It enhances the employer value proposition and brand in a competitive talent market.
- It appeals to employees interested in continuous learning and increases the human capital assets of an organization.
- It acts as an incentive and total rewards benefit to employees.
- It is a cost-effective approach to develop internal talent and promote skills development.
- It can be used as part of a performance improvement plan.

Developing a tailored learning strategy that incorporates the current and future needs of the business is an important way for HR leaders to add value to the company.

There are several ways for learning to occur within an organization. The main components of learning within a training and development strategy are formal training, informal learning, and knowledge management.

Knowledge management is the ability to create, use, and share information within an organization. This information can take the form of explicit (documented), implicit (know-how), or tacit (personal and experiential) knowledge. The systems and processes an organization uses to manage and transfer information are important to develop human capital assets and improve business performance.

Informal learning is learner-led and unstructured, and involves actions and doing. Instead of featuring a dedicated training event, informal learning's breadth, depth, and duration are driven by the employee. Informal learning can be motivated by a desire to develop longer-term skills, and can take the form of on-the-job learning, unplanned and casual interactions, networking and mentoring, and feedback from customers, former employees, and social media channels.

Summarize the methods change practitioners can use to successfully implement training.

Define instructional design and list some of the common models.

Describe the ADDIE model and identify the five steps it describes.

Describe Merrill's principles of instruction and identify the five principles it describes.

List the steps of Gagne's nine events of instruction.

Summarize Bloom's taxonomy model.

Instructional design, also known as instructional system design, is the systematic approach to designing, developing, and delivering training programs and materials in a consistent and reliable manner. This process helps outline the activities that steer the development of learning and helps to communicate its purpose and reason. The goal of instructional design is to analyze learning needs and develop improved learning experiences. Four popular instructional design models are:

- The ADDIE model
- Merrill's principles of instruction
- Gagne's nine events of instruction
- Bloom's taxonomy

Change practitioners are responsible for creating a change-positive culture that engages employees at all levels. Important knowledge, skills, and abilities needed to be successful in these roles include understanding how to think creatively, communicate effectively, distill complex topics into simple and digestible formats, and coach leaders and employees through all the changes that lead to desired business outcomes and behaviors.

Organizational learning can be delivered using a variety of methods: in-person or online, cohort or instructor-led, e-learning, videos, workbooks, and more. The right approach will incorporate the learning needs of participants, overall business objectives, and desired learning outcomes. Thinking through how best to design and deliver training allows HR leaders to use design principles to optimize impact.

After training is completed, creating continued opportunities to recall, share, and apply knowledge helps enhance learning. Creating ongoing interactions between learners and content, between learners and instructors, and between learners and other learners, can successfully promote learning and knowledge development long after a training event is finished. In addition, creating communities of practice (CoPs)—groups of people who share a passion, skill, or interest for something and learn to do it better by working together regularly—is an effective way to reinforce training and increase engagement on a topic.

This framework leverages five principles when it comes to solving problems and completing tasks:

- Learning starts when participants must solve real-world problems they can relate to.
- Activating existing knowledge is important to connect to new information.
- Encouraging learners to demonstrate knowledge using a mix of visuals and storytelling helps with retention.
- Learning is enhanced when participants apply the knowledge or skill in practice and solve problems.
- Learning should be integrated through discussion, application, and sharing of new knowledge.

The **ADDIE model** is a set of instructional design guidelines commonly used by organizations to develop human resource development (HRD) programs. "ADDIE" stands for the model's five steps: **analyze, design, develop, implement**, and **evaluate**. This is a systematic approach where each step of the process has outcomes that feed into the next step. Some critical activities include conducting a needs assessment, determining participant readiness for training, creating a learning environment, ensuring effective knowledge transfer as part of the training, developing an evaluation approach, selecting and using a training method, and monitoring and evaluating the effectiveness of the training.

The ADDIE model is commonly used in HRD because it is a simple but effective way of creating a training program. It can also be applied to a variety of fields and is not limited to training programs.

This framework includes six dimensions of cognitive learning, starting with the simplest at the bottom and moving to the most complex at the top. This model guides the learner past lower levels of knowledge and recall, to deeper areas of understanding, application, and evaluation of impact. This process can foster creative solutions, with new information generated by moving through the levels.

Each of these models has strengths, opportunities, flaws, and weaknesses. Depending on the learning objectives and desired outcomes, one or more elements of each model may be appropriate to use. HR professionals should be familiar with a range of instructional design methods to present the best solution based on business needs.

This framework takes a behaviorist approach to learning using the following steps:

- Gain attention by asking thought-provoking questions to engage the learner.
- Inform the learner of objectives, desired outcomes, and methods of measuring success.
- Stimulate recall of prior learning to utilize existing knowledge as a foundation to build on.
- Present the content in easy-to-digest and consumable chunks of information.
- Provide learner guidance with discussions, case studies, and other instructional support materials.
- Elicit performance with activities that prompt recall, utilization, and analysis of information.
- Provide feedback immediately to reinforce knowledge.
- Assess performance to test the knowledge and understanding against established criteria.
- Enhance retention and transfer to job with job aids and other strategies.

Diagram the dimensions of Bloom's Taxonomy.

Explain why it is important to perform a needs analysis before designing a training program.

Define a person needs analysis.

Define an organization needs analysis.

Define a training needs analysis.

Describe how to develop a training program and its importance.

It is important for an organization to perform a needs analysis before designing a training program for several different reasons. First, an organization should accurately identify problems. Second, even if a particular problem is known prior to the analysis, it can be difficult to identify the cause of that problem. Third, and most importantly, it is impossible to design an effective training program without first identifying the specific knowledge, skills, and abilities required to achieve goals or to correct a problem. A **needs analysis** can be an essential part of the training development process because it helps to identify and detail problems so possible solutions can be found.

There are a variety of steps that might be taken during a needs analysis, but most analyses begin by collecting data related to the performance of each part of the organization. This information is usually gathered from surveys, interviews, observations, skill assessments, performance appraisals, and so on. Once this information is collected, problems are identified within specific areas of the organization, and solutions are proposed. Advantages and disadvantages of each solution are then identified, and the plan that seems to provide the greatest benefit for the lowest cost is chosen.

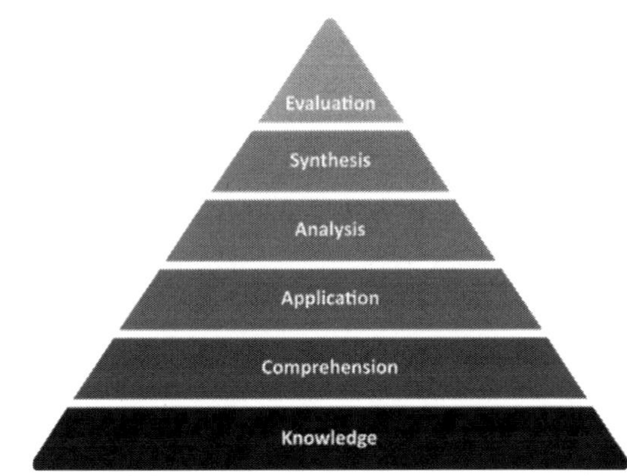

The **organization** needs analysis is conducted to ensure that the training is aligned with the overall business strategy, and that there are adequate resources and support available for training.

A **person** needs analysis is a type of needs analysis that determines several key items. The person analysis will determine how an employee performs a task compared to the expectation. Not all individuals within the organization will require training, so the person analysis establishes which specific employees need training or development. Once individuals are identified for training, the type of training will be selected.

Training improves performance for employees and organizations. Understanding how to develop, organize, and deliver training promotes continuous learning and is a competitive advantage that contributes to business growth. HR professionals tasked with developing training programs and demonstrating value to business leaders should:

- Conduct a needs assessment.
- Understand the characteristics of the learners and the organization.
- Choose appropriate training methods and delivery techniques.

A **training** needs analysis is completed to determine what gaps may exist in the actual knowledge, skills, and abilities in a role versus the desired levels. The difference between the actual competency and the standard will determine what training may be required.

Explain why training may be necessary and how to determine appropriate training program goals.

Explain how to choose an appropriate training method and how technology impacts it.

Describe a traditional classroom training delivery format.

Summarize on-the-job training and its advantages and disadvantages.

Explain what is meant by e-learning or virtual learning.

Describe what is meant by blended learning or hybrid format.

Choosing the appropriate training methods for an organization should start with a needs assessment. A needs assessment is a systematic assessment of the roles, individuals, and business to determine the characteristics and needs of the intended audience.

Technology has transformed training and development and provides new ways for organizations to help employees learn. Traditionally, in-house training programs were in high demand: content was created by internal teams with or without the help of external partners. Today, there are a number of development strategies that can be used to train, re-skill, and upskill existing teams. A few of these methods include the following.

The need to deliver training can stem from a number of scenarios: hiring new employees, rolling out a new product, entering or exiting a new market, or changing policy. Conducting a thorough needs analysis ensures that the right program is designed by revealing what exists and what needs to change, and identifying any challenges that could impact successful implementation.

Understanding the type of learners in an organization and any unique needs helps to ensure that all training goals are appropriate and that the overall training programs are delivered successfully. Characteristics such as where employees work and are located, translation and accessibility needs, stakeholders' needs, and legal and regulatory requirements will impact the scope of the training plan.

On-the-job training (OJT) is usually provided by managers or supervisors utilizing real-time demonstration of the material or equipment the employee will be using to complete job tasks. This hands-on approach is sometimes more effective than lecturing or a theoretical approach. Seeing and being allowed to perform the desired function is a simple and cost-effective method for learning. This method also allows for immediate feedback and helps to ensure the employee is immediately productive.

However, there can be disadvantages to OJT. First, the person teaching may not be a certified trainer, but rather someone who knows how the work needs to be accomplished. Teaching requires clear communication and patience, and not everyone possesses necessary teaching skills. Second, another reason for OJT is to get the new employee up to speed quickly, but in doing so, there could be safety issues and the potential for accidents. This is especially true of high-risk jobs. Lastly, OJT could be distracting to coworkers, creating work disturbances and causing lack of concentration, especially in a space-constrained environment.

A traditional classroom training is conducted in a teaching space and allows for face-to-face instruction. This mode of training can take place internally at an employer's work site, externally at a training facility, or possibly at an industry conference. Classroom training offers many options to deploy multiple learning modalities. To begin, a classroom can be conducive to teaching new information to a small or large number of students. A classroom presentation can be made lecture-style, with or without visual aids; or it can include demonstrations of material, allowing for multiple formats to teach information. If the group is small enough, classroom training can be an environment for interactive discussion, whereby the instructor gauges students understanding and immediately changes course if needed. Depending on the training, classroom training can permit employees to interact with one another, thereby enhancing the learning experience. Lastly, a classroom environment provides a human element that is challenging to capture in other training delivery formats.

A blended learning or hybrid format combines multiple methods of delivering training material. Research suggests that a mix of learning strategies and formats might be more effective than one single method. Typically, blended or hybrid learning involves face-to-face, traditional classroom instruction combined with an online, technological component that might also give the student control over their pace of learning. The following are two examples of blended or hybrid learning:

- A course with synchronous learning in a virtual setting using video, as well as independent, web-based, self-paced learning modules that complement classroom instruction.
- A training program that involves a web-based book with case studies, as well as traditional face-to-face classroom instruction coupled with a mobile application for simulation exercises.

Blended learning or hybrid instruction has many advantages: it works well with different student learning styles, enables both independent and collective learning, supports learning in a global workforce, and provides scheduling flexibility. On the other hand, there are some concerns that must be addressed; for example, more advanced planning is necessary, students need to be organized in how they will attend, students potentially need more motivation with this format, there may be feelings of not being connected and needing more encouragement, and development costs can be higher. This integrated, blended learning environment is constantly evolving as technology affords the organization more options.

E-learning, also known as virtual learning, is a training delivery format that permits students to learn via a form that utilizes technology. E-learning can take a number of different formats, including web-based, mobile computer applications, and virtual classrooms. E-learning can be synchronous, in which the instructor and students are interacting in real time. Alternatively, e-learning can be asynchronous, enabling students to access the same training and related materials on demand at different days and times.

There are many benefits to using e-learning, such as delivering a large volume of information quickly, assisting globalization efforts through virtual learning, scheduling flexibility, and cost effectiveness. However, there are considerations that should be examined, including technology constraints and user access, concerns about intellectual property, lack of face-to-face interaction possibly causing uneasiness with students, and the potentially significant costs involved in training development.

Summarize some of the different delivery styles for training programs.

Explain some of the considerations when deciding between in-house and third-party training programs.

Describe change management and how it relates to learning.

Define learning management systems and their advantages.

List some examples of external factors that act as forces for change and how they affect an organization.

Describe how HR leaders can help facilitate individual change.

A critical question that comes up when assessing the learning needs of an organization is whether the training should be developed and delivered in-house or through a third party. Deciding whether all elements or specific components of the instructional design will be outsourced will help to clarify the value proposition of the training program. Companies can choose to partner with external vendors on specific elements ranging from content creation to design, illustration, voice-over, translation, and accessibility services.

Some important considerations when deciding whether to insource or outsource learning content include:

- Type of training (e.g., legally required, role-specific, business-specific)
- Length and duration of training (how often learners will need to retest)
- Location of training audience (whether multiple languages are needed)
- Data privacy and accessibility (single sign-on or externally hosted site)
- Trademark and copyright considerations
- Feedback mechanisms needed to get input on the end users' experience

Learning is the acquisition of knowledge through experience, leading to lasting behavior change. Change refers to the adoption of a new idea or behavior. The consistent application of learning as knowledge creates change. Change management refers to the collective approach to initiating, organizing, implementing, and supporting organizational change for individuals, teams, and entire groups. A good way to think about change is to examine what happens when someone learns something new. When done consistently and repeatedly, this kind of change can be an accelerant for business transformation and a source of competitive advantage.

Individual change is at the center of everything that is achieved within organizations. Many change scenarios require employees to learn new things on their own and come together in teams and networks to apply those learnings in new and innovative ways. Leaders play a crucial role in guiding individuals and teams through changes that facilitate business transformation. Managers play a dual role of creating urgency with individuals around a big opportunity, while managing themselves through the change as well. The more tools a leader has to influence behavior, the more successful they will be in leading teams through change.

There are a variety of models and frameworks used for each approach that offer insight to leaders on the impact of organizational change. Understanding the different approaches and the advantages and disadvantages associated with each style can help HR professionals provide solutions that meet the needs of many types of teams and businesses.

Anticipating resistance to change and understanding the roots of concerns is another powerful way that HR leaders can support change management efforts. Most individual struggles fall into one or more versions of "I don't understand it," "I don't like it," or "I don't need it."

How work gets done continues to change thanks to macro trends toward globalization, digitization, and changes brought on by the COVID-19 pandemic. With continued focus on collaboration and working across team and cultural boundaries, HR professionals should be well versed in multiple approaches to increase training effectiveness. Some popular styles include:

- **Role play**: This allows the learner to act and speak like the character they are trying to portray. Benefits include practice, which builds experience, and more chances for real-time feedback, which can be applied to enhance performance.
- **Facilitation**: This allows learners to be introduced to the content by a facilitator who guides learners through the content, asks questions, and steers the overall discussion. This style promotes real-time feedback.
- **Case studies**: This involves reviewing a real-life historical situation to learn from others' lived experiences. This can occur in person, online, or in a blended learning situation. This approach gives learners perspective and insights into unique challenges and allows for low-stakes learning opportunities.
- **Games and simulations**: These bring the strategies, rules, and social experiences of game play into a learning setting. This style incorporates digital and gamification tools into learning content and delivers training in a way that increases engagement with learners.

The increased use of e-learning—training that is delivered through an online platform via computers and mobile devices—means organizations must invest in software that helps to create, manage, distribute, and track employee training. Learning management systems (LMSs) are often used in business settings to deliver online training and track employee progress. An LMS allows organizations to harness analytics to evaluate training offerings, enhance the learner experience, and increase effectiveness of training programs. A well-integrated LMS will complement career development efforts by delivering relevant learning content to strong performers, employees new to the company or new in their roles, or those looking to re-skill for the future.

A huge benefit of investing in an LMS is the ability to pull reporting and analytics that provide useful measurements around spending on learning, utilization, compliance, and engagement with enterprise learning systems.

An essential ingredient to successfully implement change is the ability of people leaders to distinguish between the external changes that occur and the concurrent intrinsic and psychological changes that affect individual employees, including change leaders. Understanding external factors that prompt change in organizations, along with individual approaches to behavior change, can equip HR teams with the knowledge they need to support leaders and businesses through change scenarios.

Change can result from businesses experiencing volatility, uncertainty, complexity, and ambiguity (VUCA) events. Most recently, COVID-19 and the pandemic ushered in a "new normal" and transformed many ways of working, including how HR teams develop and deliver business-critical training and learning in a remote manner. Many companies quickly adapted their operating models, supply chains, vendor relationships, and communication models to engage customers and consumers through years of uncertainty and ambiguity. Other global trends that have precipitated change recently include:

- Globalization and increasingly complex operating environments impacting approaches to risk management and compliance, talent pipelines, vendor relationships, and business models
- Digital transformation and technology enabling advanced solutions and tools for employees and customers
- Emphasis on diversity, equity, and inclusion initiatives including employee resource groups, employee well-being resources, and accessibility tools for the differently abled
- Shifts in attitudes on total rewards advocating for more pay transparency, increased parental leave, debt support, and mental wellness

Summarize the four approaches to understanding how change impacts individuals.

Describe the elements of the change management process.

Explain the importance of continuous progress in training programs and how to measure this progress.

Describe how to evaluate the effectiveness of training programs and its importance.

Describe Kirkpatrick's four-level evaluation model.

Describe how a learning management system can be used to evaluate training program effectiveness.

Taking practical steps to assess the readiness of individuals for a planned change can help leaders prepare to manage across the organization. Any behavior changes or project plans that require employees to do something new or different will require a few steps:

1. Create a burning case for change with leaders, decision makers, and key stakeholders to collaborate and gain alignment, commitment, and support for the change.
2. Define the future state and identify the needs of the organization: list the desired behaviors, performance, processes, and initiatives that will help to realize the strategic opportunity.
3. Do a gap analysis to measure how often the desired behaviors are currently used across the organization.
4. Create short-term milestones and celebrate achievement in a public way to increase motivation and buy-in.
5. Develop robust communication plans for stakeholders, with key messages, job aids, checklists, and other tools. Communicate about the impact of the change and solicit feedback about employee sentiment on the change.
6. Leave room in future phases to incorporate stakeholder feedback to deepen buy-in and support.

Throughout each of these steps, leaders should offer ongoing support in the form of additional resources and training to provide information about the need for change and reinforce desired outcomes throughout the change journey. To be effective, training must align with and reinforce the strategic goals of the business. Using both quantitative measures (e.g., surveys) and qualitative measures (e.g., focus groups) will provide a more comprehensive view of how the change is being received. Offering resources to increase understanding around change, soliciting real-time and continuous feedback about change, and incorporating end-user feedback will boost support and limit any disruptive impacts.

To understand how change impacts people, it is important to know these four schools of thought:

- The **behavioral approach** focuses on individuals influencing other individuals with reward and punishment mechanisms. If the desired results are not achieved, an analysis of the individual's behavior is conducted to better understand non-achievement. A downside of this approach is that it relies solely on observable behavior to measure progress.
- The **cognitive approach** focuses on individuals' capacity for problem-solving and asserts that emotions and reactions are a result of how things are perceived. This view maintains that attitudes and behavior are driven by how individuals view the world. This approach centers on the ability to change how people think. A drawback of this approach is underestimating the inner emotional world of individuals and the impact that it has on their outlook and ability to work through change.
- The **psychodynamic approach** explains that individuals go through a range of internal emotions in response to external circumstances. This approach is useful to understand reactions to a change and how to handle them. This approach is criticized for not accounting for an individual's ability to think, act, and control their own behavior.
- The **humanistic approach** takes a holistic view of individuals as more than their thoughts, emotions, and behaviors and focuses on the ability to choose. A drawback of this approach is that it requires an individual to have a minimum amount of verbal fluency, intellect, and confidence to express themselves.

Evaluating and measuring the effectiveness of training programs has many benefits. It supports learning effectiveness, helps to align training investment to business strategy, and engages participants in the design and delivery process. Many leaders view training evaluation as the end of learning, but it actually serves as the beginning of the continuous improvement process. Successful measurement results in feedback that is incorporated into the future content and structure of training events and can boost training efficacy. Soliciting feedback from participants—and actively incorporating those inputs—builds trust and drives engagement, which are key drivers of retention.

Possibly the most common method of evaluation is Kirkpatrick's training effectiveness model, which has been successfully used across a range of businesses and industries. This framework can be used to evaluate formal and informal training events, which makes it ideal for numerous scenarios. The model consists of four levels of response to a training or learning event:

- Level 1: Reaction—How did participants respond to the training?
- Level 2: Learning—How much did participants learn from the training, and did their skills improve?
- Level 3: Behavior—How have participants applied the training in their work?
- Level 4: Results—What has improved or been impacted as a result of the training?

Over time, the original work has been expanded into what is called the New World Kirkpatrick model. This version turns the model upside down; it emphasizes identifying level 4 (results) up front and focusing on the collective efforts of interested parties to achieve a return on stakeholder expectations.

Implementing change in an organization should trigger a continuous process that focuses on how to get change to stick. A desired outcome for most changes is implementing the new behavior as status quo, which involves an ongoing campaign of outreach, engagement, and communication. An important way to measure progress is to establish metrics and assess whether desired outcomes are occurring in the organization. By identifying forward-looking measures for how things will operate in the future, HR leaders can use data to confirm that the right changes are taking hold.

Change leaders must tune in to the environment to monitor how change is taking hold across the organization. It is important to build coalitions of passionate supporters—and detractors—to get feedback on how change is being communicated across teams. When possible, it is also helpful to reinforce key messages with this group, remove barriers, and empower them to go back to their teams with information and updates on the change. Many teams leverage these networks of change agents and change champions to build trust at the grassroots levels and drive implementation.

Change management plans are all about deconstructing change into small steps. Understanding what motivates individuals, and how they respond to change, can equip business and HR leaders with perspectives and tools that drive results that directly impact the bottom line.

Other tools for evaluating training effectiveness include reports and participant feedback, which can be used at each level to obtain valuable insight into the success of any training offering.

A popular tool that supports all levels of training evaluation is a learning management system (LMS) software solution with built-in functionality to collect training feedback, aggregate evaluations, and offer reporting capability for deeper insights. A strong LMS can streamline how HR leaders approach training evaluation.

A variety of tools exist to help measure training efficacy, and certain measurement tools are more suitable for certain levels. Donald Kirkpatrick introduced a **four-level training evaluation model** for planning, evaluating, and preserving. The four levels of the Kirkpatrick evaluation model are as follows:

- Level 1 training evaluations are the most common, and they can be relatively easy and fast compared to other methods. Surveys that measure participants' knowledge, skills, attitudes, and reactions are common for this level.
- Level 2 training evaluations measure learning. These methods must be both reliable and valid to be useful. They can take the form of pre- and post-tests and include self-assessments on how knowledge has been applied. Providing job aids, quick reference guides, and other tools to use after training is another best practice to enhance learning.
- Level 3 training evaluations measure how information is applied. Data collection at this stage can take the form of self-reporting by the learner (often surveys and questionnaires), on-the-job observation to see if new skills are being applied, or obtaining 360-degree feedback from leaders, teammates, and business partners on changes in behavior. While it may be difficult to prove that behavior changes resulted directly from training, a variety of evaluation methods and feedback can home in on drivers of change.
- Level 4 training evaluations measure results and can be the most time-consuming and expensive to implement. These can look like focus groups, strategic interviews, and observations.

Explain why it is important to perform a needs analysis before designing a training program.

Explain the purpose of a pre- and post-training evaluation.

Explain why an organization should conduct participant training surveys.

Summarize the rationale and procedures in an after-action review.

Explain the importance of pay structure.

Describe the process of creating a pay structure.

The end goal of any training is to have the participants learn and apply the new knowledge or material in the most effective manner possible. Information obtained in a **pre-training survey** can help ensure the training meets expected learning outcomes, gauge student expectations, and provide information about the students' abilities and their learning preferences. The data gathered from the pre-training evaluation will help the instructor customize the training to improve learning. Pre-training survey questions need to be tailored for the intended audience—the right questions need to be asked in the right format. This can vary tremendously depending on the training and the participants. The objective is to have a clear assessment of the participant's skill-based knowledge before the training.

Meanwhile, the questions asked in a **post-training survey** should measure whether the content taught was learned and understood. Frequently, skills-based questions in the post-training survey will be similar to those asked in the pre-training survey. This is done intentionally to measure whether the information taught was truly learned, meaning there should be improved scores in the post-training evaluation. Organizations will typically do another survey anywhere from 30 days to 6 months after the training to gauge training effectiveness.

It is important for an organization to perform a needs analysis before designing a training program for several reasons. First, an organization can accurately identify problems. Second, even if a particular problem is known prior to the analysis, it can be difficult to identify the cause of that problem. Third, and most importantly, it is impossible to design an effective training program without first identifying the specific knowledge, skills, and abilities required to achieve goals or correct a problem. A needs analysis can be an essential part of the training development process because it helps to identify and inform about problems so that possible solutions can be found.

The term **"after-action review"** was originally used by the military after field operations as a structured approach to identify the group's strengths, weaknesses, and areas for improvement based on real-life events. Many companies, including GE, BP, and Motorola, use an after-action review to improve their operations. This approach is focused on three primary questions:
- What was supposed to happen, and what actually happened?
- What went well, and why?
- What can be improved, and how?

An after-action review is a structured debriefing that allows an organization to gain insights and knowledge that will enable it to learn from past missteps or mistakes so they are not repeated. Moreover, this reflective, knowledge-is-power method can correct situations that were not ideal and/or help replicate situations that were handled well. The following are the typical processes and objectives when conducting an after-action review:
- Conduct the after-action review as soon as possible after the event so it is fresh in everyone's memory.
- Include everyone involved and set ground rules so that honest opinions are offered with respect to all present.
- Ask all structured questions (listed above) and document responses for lessons learned.
- Document a report detailing all learned strengths, weaknesses, and areas for improvement or areas to be replicated.
- Implement needed changes immediately.

Training is an essential function for almost any organization. Sometimes, in cases of sexual harassment, corporate policy, discriminatory practice and legislation, etc., it can even be mandatory. In other cases, it is a necessity because information and technology are constantly advancing. Additionally, companies spend a considerable amount of money on training and should see a return on their investment. Therefore, organizations should always evaluate and assess training effectiveness.

One of the ways to assess training is through a training participant survey. This type of survey involves asking employees questions to better gauge how they view the effectiveness of the training. Individuals have different learning styles and learn in many different ways. Their input can help an organization improve future training programs. The survey is usually done electronically and can vary enormously depending on the training needs and makeup of the organization. Generally, questions will either be quantitative, meaning they are evaluated on a numeric scale, or qualitative, meaning they require verbiage and/or accurate responses. Possible questions might be:
- What was your overall impression of the training program?
- What particular part of the training did you feel was the most useful?
- On a scale of 1 to 5, with 1 being the worst and 5 the best, answer the following questions:
  - How would you rate this training program?
  - How would you rate the instructor?
  - How would you rate the technology used?
  - How would you rate your ability to immediately use the information learned?

Methods of creating a pay structure can vary greatly, but most organizations begin the process by conducting a job evaluation for each position. A **job evaluation** is the process whereby the value of a job to the organization is determined—it is how a job's worth is established. Once all positions are evaluated and assigned a value, they are categorized based on their importance to the organization. The organization will usually gather information from salary surveys to determine the market median for each category and the wages an individual would receive at the midpoint of a similar pay category for another organization. Finally, using all of this information as a guide, a **pay range** is developed for each category.

Pay ranges can be a challenge because this is a very fluid process. Occasionally, an employee is paid above the range maximum or below the range minimum. When an employee is paid above a range maximum, it is called a **"red-circle rate"** and could mean that an employer's pay range is below the market value and should be researched to remain competitive. If the pay rate is below the range minimum, it is called a **"green-circle rate"** and should also be re-examined.

Pay structure is the way an organization groups jobs and defines the compensation associated with a collection of jobs. Pay structure is critical because every organization needs qualified and talented individuals to build and run a business. One of the best ways to obtain and retain good talent is through a fair and attractive pay structure. Additionally, as in most areas of HR, pay structure needs to demonstrate that an organization has fair and consistent policies surrounding all aspects of pay. This structure will help an organization meet necessary compliance requirements, as well as clearly demonstrate fair practices related to pay opportunities for all employees.

One of the most important considerations in pay structure is the balance between internal and external pay equity. Internal pay equity is how an employee's pay compares to the pay of others in similar positions within the organization. External pay equity is the comparison of pay to similar jobs outside the organization. A balance indicates the pay is fair, which will help attract new employees and also help retain existing employees in the organization.

Describe pay grades and banding.

Describe a traditional salary structure.

Summarize a broadband salary structure and rationale for usage.

Explain how a market-based pay structure is organized.

Explain the purpose of variable pay.

Describe pay compression.

A **traditional salary structure** could have multiple pay ranges that correlate to differences in a position. The way it typically works is that a new employee will be offered a salary on the lower end of the pay range, and then hopefully advance to a higher pay range depending on their performance evaluation or other means of evaluating the employee. The benefit of an organization using a traditional salary structure is that it provides the organization and its employees an easy-to-understand "ladder" or hierarchical system for an employee to advance or be promoted from one pay grade to another. Typically, an organization will first set the minimum and maximum salary range for each grouping. Then, based on the number of groupings, the organization will figure out the logical number of pay grades in their salary structure.

A **pay grade** refers to a compensation job grouping, by level, with similar responsibilities, authority, and experience. This grouping means that within an organization, similar jobs have approximately the same relative value and are therefore paid at similar rates within a pay range. Some compensation structures break out pay grades or ranges into separate **bands** (or levels) so the company can maintain pay equity and stay within budget. This is done by conducting a job analysis and grouping titles into families. For example, those that fall into the first pay grade may have a pay band of $20,000 to $35,000, the second pay grade may have a band of $30,000 to $50,000, and the third pay grade may have a band of $50,000 to $100,000. Jobs may also be evaluated and ranked based upon overall responsibilities and worth to the organization.

Although pay bands are broken out based upon job duty and skill level, it is important to recognize whether the company tends to lead, lag, or match current market rates. Matching or leading the market is best for recruitment and retention. The sizes of pay bands tend to grow as you move up the managerial ladder, with executives having the largest pay levels.

A **market-based pay structure** can be thought of as a combination of traditional and broadband structures, except market-based pay is a pay scale based on what similar employers in similar geographic locations pay employees. In other words, appropriate pay is determined by an employer evaluating data from various sources in the job market that summarize pay for similar jobs. Sources include the US Bureau of Labor Statistics and some private companies that offer salary surveys for a fee. Like traditional and broadband, the market-based pay structure also has a pay range for specific jobs. However, what usually happens is that the pay range, minimum to maximum, is too slim to be competitive with similar jobs in the external market, while the salary range is usually too high, like the broadband structure. A large majority of businesses utilize a market-based pay structure in their organization.

A **broadband salary structure** takes multiple pay grades that only have a modest difference between the minimum and maximum pay scale and combines them into a single band with a much broader difference in the spread. In effect, the organization is collapsing multiple ranges in order to obtain a larger spread between the minimum and maximum point for a salary range. An organization might use a broadband salary structure if they wish to remove hierarchical levels and thereby limit the levels of management, a process sometimes referred to as "flattening" an organization. For example, an organization may have had 10 levels of management, with a narrow salary range in each level. They then decide to adopt a broadband salary structure and reduce the levels from 10 to 5, thereby also allowing the organization to increase the difference in the salary range. Existing employees are then moved to the most appropriate level within the five options. Companies may also choose a broadband salary structure in a large organization if managing too many pay grades becomes complex and difficult to equitably administer.

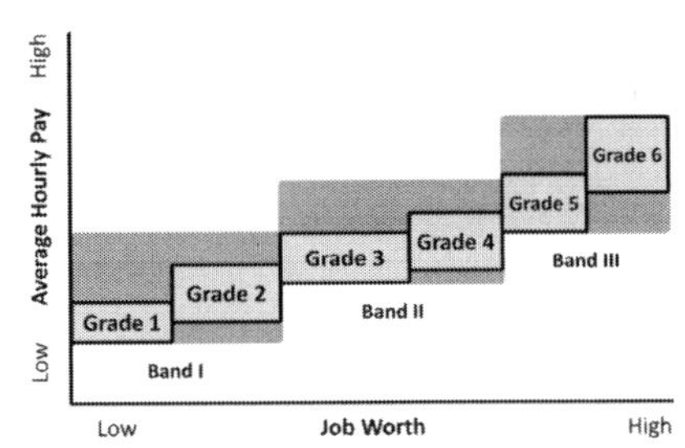

Pay compression occurs when a senior employee has a salary that is only slightly more, or in some cases less, than a new hire in the same position. This is a situation in which beginning salaries for new hires are too close to the salaries for existing employees in the same job. In some cases, it is not exactly the same job—this could also occur if a new hire makes more money than their manager. Pay compression can be the cause of high turnover and employee disengagement. Causes of pay compression may include the following:

- An organization increases wages to attract new hires and doesn't adjust wages for existing employees according to market changes.
- Internal compensation is not aligned with real-world market salary data.
- There are issues with existing organizational pay grades, levels, and bands.

The answer to pay compression is easy, but its implementation and fallout are challenging. The answer is to adjust the inequities and pay employees fair market-value wages. This is a costly proposition for most organizations, but if they do not adjust wages accordingly, they risk losing good workers and facing the challenges and costs that come with replacing them.

Variable pay is employee pay that changes based on predetermined parameters or goals set by an employer. Variable pay is most often used as a monetary incentive to achieve business objectives and reward employees, and is usually a supplement to base salary or wages. An organization that wants to use variable pay to incentivize behavior or performance can accomplish this goal based on criteria such as sales revenue, customer satisfaction scores, percentage increase in clients, and pieces produced. Variable pay is frequently either a dollar amount or percentage based on target objectives and is included in an employee's overall compensation plan. The following are some examples of how variable pay might work:

- An electrician paid hourly could be paid $30 extra for every referral made.
- An account executive could be paid a salary and, for every quarter that his or her team exceeds their sales objective by 10 percent, could receive an additional $5,000.
- An assembly line worker who exceeds his or her pieces built per hour by 10 percent or more (with no defects) could receive an extra $100 per day.

Summarize four common methods used to evaluate and classify jobs.

Describe pay adjustments and their importance.

Define differential pay and demonstrate how it is calculated.

Define the cost-of-living adjustment (COLA) and demonstrate how it is calculated.

Describe the attributes of bonus pay.

Summarize merit pay and what differentiates it from other incentive pay programs.

Pay adjustments are not generally required by law, except when necessary to match minimum wage increases. However, pay adjustments are an important part of a company's compensation strategy for positions at all levels.

Employees expect to be rewarded with pay increases as time goes by as a reward for their hard work, loyalty, and contributions. Without pay increases, employees may feel unappreciated—which can negatively impact job performance, engagement, and retention. A company also needs to consider the fact that the cost of living changes over time, a factor that can reduce the overall value of employee compensation.

It is common for companies to consider pay adjustments on an annual basis, though some employers do so more or less frequently.

- For salaried employees, pay adjustments are ordinarily awarded as a percentage of current compensation, though a company can opt to award a specific dollar amount.
- For hourly workers, an employer may opt to adjust pay as a flat per-hour increase or as a percentage of the current hourly rate.

Job evaluation is the process a company uses to identify the relative worth (in terms of monetary value) of each position.

Common methods used to evaluate and classify jobs include:

- **Ranking method**—Ranking begins by listing all an organization's jobs in order, from the highest value or difficulty to the lowest value or difficulty. Those that have the highest value or difficulty receive the highest pay, with compensation adjusted accordingly as the level of value or difficulty decreases.
- **Classification method**—Rather than starting with individual jobs, classification involves establishing multiple pay grades and writing a broad description for each grade. Next, each job description is compared to the description of each grade and assigned to the closest match.
- **Point method**—The point method involves identifying various compensable factors that will be evaluated to determine how much individual jobs should pay. Points are assigned for each compensable factor and compared to benchmark positions within the company.
- **Factor comparison method**—Factor comparison involves evaluating each job against a benchmark position in relation to a set group of five predetermined factors, which are usually defined as skill level, responsibility, mental requirements, physical requirements, and working conditions.

Ranking and classification are non-quantitative classification methods, while the point method and factor comparison method are quantitative.

A **cost-of-living adjustment** (COLA) is designed to counteract and stabilize inflation by declaring a percentage increase in Social Security and supplemental income. Usually, a COLA is equal to the percentage rise in the consumer price index for urban wage earners and clerical workers (CPI-W) for a predefined period of time, a calculation that frequently aligns with the calculation for inflation. For example, if a person received $20,000 in Social Security and the COLA was evaluated at 3.1%, then their benefits would be $20,620 for the year. COLA began in 1975 in response to high inflation and is evaluated every year. The Social Security Administration uses COLAs to protect compensation-based benefits from inflation.

Differential pay is when an organization pays an employee an extra wage for working undesirable shifts or hours. This could mean working through the night or maybe on the weekend or a holiday. Organizations are not legally obligated to offer differential pay; rather, they offer it to incentivize people to work those shifts. However, if a worker works over 40 hours in a week, regardless of shift, then they are entitled to overtime pay according to the Fair Labor Standards Act (FLSA). Most employers offer differential pay as a percentage. For example, suppose XYZ Supermarket offers 20% differential for the overnight shift, and the normal day rate of pay is $15 an hour. Multiplying 20% by the normal rate of pay ($15 \times 0.20 = 3$) indicates that the differential would be an additional $3 per hour, meaning the worker doing the overnight shift would earn $18 an hour.

Merit pay is money awarded to an employee, via a base pay increase, based on predetermined and performance-related goals. The FLSA does not require or manage merit pay; the management and distribution of merit pay is between the employer and the employee. The overarching goal of merit pay is to motivate employees to meet and hopefully exceed individual predetermined goals. A merit pay program can drive individuals to be more productive and hence an organization more successful. The difference between merit pay and other incentive pay programs (variable, commission, etc.) is that it is incorporated into an employee's base salary rather than being a one-time occurrence. Merit increases can vary based on the organization and circumstances, but typically are under 5 percent of base salary.

There are many advantages to merit pay, such as monetarily rewarding high performers, assisting with the retention of top talent, and differentiating individual contributions versus team contributions to company goals. On the other hand, there are some issues to be aware of when administering a merit pay program, including making sure there are predefined, clear, measurable performance objectives, as well as managing merit awards in a fair, consistent manner.

Bonus pay is similar to variable pay in that an employee is paid a sum of money based on criteria set by the organization, but not necessarily linked to a clear objective. For example, at the end of the year, an organization might pay employees a bonus, perhaps a percentage of pay or just a lump sum not based on wages. This type of bonus could be offered because the business or the individual achieved certain goals, or the bonus could be made at a manager's discretion to reward the employee(s). Discretion-based bonuses could be given at any interval of time—perhaps by a manager when an employee successfully handled the closing of a deal. Additionally, a bonus could be shared among an entire department, region, team, etc., for a goal achieved or any other valued display of work.

There is only a subtle difference between bonus pay and variable pay. Bonuses may be linked to an achievement of predetermined metrics or factors, such as a holiday bonus or manager discretion bonus. Generally, bonuses reward past activities or achievements, whereas variable pay encourages future performance.

Describe incentives and some of the various approaches used.

List some of the approaches used in incentive compensation.

Summarize service awards and list some of the common types.

Explain how to develop a compensation and benefits strategy.

Summarize how to conduct an internal market analysis.

Summarize how to conduct an external market analysis.

Examples of commonly used approaches to incentive compensation include:

- **Skill-based pay**—A company seeking to have highly trained employees who are prepared for multiple roles in the company may incentivize employees to master new skills.
- **Shift differentials**—Companies with multiple shifts may incentivize employees to accept hard-to-staff shifts with a higher rate of pay for those time slots.
- **Profit sharing**—Some organizations have structured incentive programs that provide profit sharing bonuses on a quarterly or annual basis.
- **Gain sharing**—A company looking for ways to decrease expenses may incentivize employees to increase efficiency by sharing cost savings with them.
- **Year-end bonus**—Some companies offer a year-end bonus to employees as a way of saying thank you for their hard work and service throughout the year.

In addition to base pay, a company may include incentives in its compensation strategy. Incentives should be strategically aligned with the company's goals and objectives, while also providing a way for employees to increase their earnings.

Some incentive programs are specific to certain types of jobs, while others may be open to all types of employees. Examples of commonly used approaches to incentive compensation include:

- **Sales commission**—Sales professionals often earn a percentage of each sale they make as part of their compensation package.
- **Customer referral**—To encourage non-sales employees to refer customers, a company may incentivize other team members by paying a finder's fee for new customers they refer.
- **Employee referral**—To boost its applicant pool, an employer may incentivize current employees by paying a bonus when an applicant they refer joins the company.
- **Signing bonus**—For hard-to-fill jobs, an employer may induce applicants to join their company by offering a signing bonus.

In developing a compensation and benefits strategy, it's important for a company to be aware of what other companies pay for similar positions, or for employees who have the skills and backgrounds that an organization needs. After all, a business must compete with other businesses not just for customers, but also for employees.

Gathering or reviewing market analysis data can help determine whether a company's compensation is similar to that of companies with whom an organization is competing for talent, or if the pay is above or below what other employers are paying. This information can be used to make a business case for keeping compensation where it is, or to support making changes such as increasing pay or adding benefits.

Service awards can also play an important role in a company's compensation strategy. A service awards program is designed to recognize employees for longevity with a company, so these programs are sometimes referred to as "years of service" awards. These awards may be tangible items or have monetary value, or both.

- **Anniversary recognition**—Some companies recognize team members on each employment anniversary with a mention in an employee newsletter, a certificate of appreciation, a thank-you note from the CEO, logo merchandise, or other items.
- **Milestone awards**—Service award programs often include larger items or more formal recognition, such as acknowledgement at the annual meeting or higher-value items, when employees reach major milestones, such as 5, 10, or 15 years.
- **Longevity pay**—Some compensation systems include longevity pay, which can be a bonus for each year of service or a step raise, which is an increase in pay automatically awarded when employees complete another year of service.

Rather than conducting a market analysis internally, it is also possible to work with external service providers to gain access to compensation data. While there are fees associated with using external service providers, it's usually possible to get information faster this way as compared to internal research.

- The company's benefits broker may be able to provide access to market analysis data about the types of benefits that employers in the same industry or size category tend to provide.
- Some third-party organizations compile salary data that they make available to employers for a fee. For example, it is possible to purchase access to federal, state, and metro-specific salary survey data and benchmarks via Compensation.BLR.com.
- For data customized to specific interests or needs, a company might engage a compensation and benefits consultant or consulting firm to conduct a custom market analysis.

Compensation-related market analysis data can be gathered via internal research, though it can be quite time-consuming to take this approach. Gathering information for this type of market analysis usually involves scouring job openings posted by companies with similar positions, as well as reviewing position-specific pay data that the Bureau of Labor Statistics (BLS)—a division of the Department of Labor (DOL)—publishes online. Websites like Payscale.com and ZipRecruiter.com can also be helpful resources for finding information on pay for certain types of positions.

Describe the advantages of working with an external service provider to develop compensation strategies.

Summarize employee benefits and their advantages.

Explain the difference between non-discretionary and discretionary benefits.

Describe the benefits of flexible benefit programs.

Describe the core concepts of pensions or retirement plans.

Describe employee stock ownership plans (ESOP) and when companies might use them.

Employee benefits are an important aspect of a company's compensation program. They add financial value to the wages and any incentives a company offers, and they meet important health and wellness needs for employees and their families.

Benefits packages usually include access to group health coverage, as well as other kinds of group benefits like dental insurance, vision plans, term life insurance, and more. Without access to group health coverage or other types of group benefits, employees who want coverage would have to purchase individual plans on the open market. Individual plans tend to be much more expensive than group plans.

In some cases, offering benefits also helps employers comply with regulatory requirements. For example, companies with 50 or more employees are subject to financial penalties if they don't offer health insurance that meets the requirements of the Patient Protection and Affordable Care Act (PPACA).

Some companies rely on their own internal resources to develop and administer their compensation strategy, while others engage outside consultants to lead this aspect of operations. In a small business, the HR manager or director, or a member of the executive team, may be responsible for compensation strategy, while the HR team in a larger organization may have one or more compensation specialists or compensation analysts on staff.

In either case, a company may opt to work with an external services provider for a special project or on an ongoing basis. This could involve contracting with an individual compensation consultant or engaging a consulting firm that offers compensation strategy services. There are several reasons it can be beneficial to work with an external service provider, including the following:

- Developing an effective compensation strategy requires time and focus. A consultant can focus solely on this one thing rather than trying to fit it in with the myriad of day-to-day compensation-related matters that require the attention of internal staff members.
- It can be difficult for an internal team member to be truly objective about compensation at the company where they work. As a third party, a consultant will bring an external and objective perspective to compensation strategy.
- Developing compensation strategy requires expertise beyond how to administer a compensation program. A consultant who specializes in compensation strategy will have not only compensation-specific expertise, but also expertise in strategic planning and bottom-line impact.

Flexible benefits are programs offered by an employer that enable an employee to select and create their own customized benefits based on their preferences. In recent years, employees have come to expect benefits that promote work-life balance and support families. To that end, an increasing number of employers offer telecommuting, flex time, and compressed work week options to help workers juggle all of life's different demands. In addition, many workplaces now offer benefits like paid parental leave and designated lactation rooms, making it easier on new parents. Additionally, some employers have started offering paid caregiver leave, which allows workers to care for parents and other relatives without worrying about their paychecks. Small and large businesses alike recognize that flexible benefits are necessary to remain competitive in the marketplace.

Benefits fit under two basic categories: non-discretionary and discretionary. **Non-discretionary** benefits are benefits that an employer must offer and are mandated under various legal statutes. These benefits can include, but are not limited to, unemployment insurance, Medicare, workers' compensation, Social Security, unpaid family medical leave, and COBRA.

Discretionary benefits are those benefits that an employer chooses to offer—and thus are not mandated by legal regulations—in order to attract and retain talent. Generally, discretionary benefits comprise three primary areas:

- **Health benefits**—This includes everything under the healthcare umbrella, including medical, dental, vision, prescription, employee assistance programs, disability insurance, and life insurance.
- **Deferred compensation**—This area includes any type of employer-offered retirement plan whereby the benefit is received at a later date than when work is performed.
- **Other** discretionary benefits—This includes perks that do not fit into health benefits or deferred compensation, such as paid time off for holidays, paid vacation time, flexible work schedule, tuition reimbursement, and childcare.

An **employee stock ownership plan** (ESOP) is created by establishing a trust into which the business makes contributions of cash or stock that are tax deductible. Employees are then granted the ability to purchase stock or allocate funds into individual employee accounts. The stock is held in an **employee stock ownership trust** (ESOT), and the business can make regular contributions, typically up to 25 percent of its annual payroll. ESOPs became popular because it is believed that employees who have an ownership interest in the business will work more diligently and also have a vested interest in its efficiency and profitability. Although this logic is debatable, many studies have shown that ESOPs do motivate employees and support business growth.

Pensions and company retirement plans fund an individual's retirement by providing deferred payments for prior services. These accounts may be funded by the employer through a variety of means. Retirement benefits are accumulated by the total amount contributed plus interest and market earnings. These defined contribution benefit plans are the traditional company-provided plans, such as 401(k)s, 403(b)s, simplified employee pensions (SEPs), SIMPLEs, and IRAs. A defined contribution benefit plan requires separate accounts for each employee participant, and funds are most often contributed by both the employee and the employer.

Some employers will implement an auto-enroll policy in which new employees are automatically enrolled and minimum contributions to the plan are withheld from payroll. The contribution rates may even automatically increase on an annual basis. However, the Pension Protection Act of 2006 provides employees with a 90-day window to opt out of these plans and recover any funds contributed on their behalf.

Summarize who is eligible for Medicare and how it is organized.

Explain the purpose of social security and its covered parties.

Visit *mometrix.com/academy* for a related video.
Enter video code: 507454

Describe managed care healthcare plans.

Describe the most common types of managed care healthcare plans.

Define the core concepts of a cafeteria plan.

List some benefits a cafeteria plan provides.

The Social Security Act was first implemented to force workers into saving a fraction of earnings for retirement and to require employers to match those funds. These funds are now withheld as a portion of the **Federal Insurance Contributions Act (FICA) payroll taxes** and regulated by the IRS. The benefits have since been extended to cover four types of insurance benefits:

- **Old age or disability benefits**—For workers who retire or become unable to work due to disability; based upon eligibility requirements
- Benefits for dependents of retired, disabled, or deceased workers—Paid to certain dependents
- **Lump-sum death benefits**—Paid to the worker's survivors
- **Medicare**—Healthcare protection provided to individuals age 65 and older, consisting of Parts A, B, and D

Medicare, established in 1965 as an amendment to the Social Security Act of 1935, is healthcare coverage primarily for people 65 years of age or older. Medicare is not dependent on income levels and is also available to individuals under age 65 who are disabled. Employers and employees contribute a percentage of salaries to fund Medicare. There are four types of Medicare coverage:

- Medicare **Part A**: This free coverage is considered mandatory for basic hospital coverage.
- Medicare **Part B**: Optional and additional medical insurance coverage for eligible individuals who pay a monthly fee.
- Medicare **Part C**: Additional healthcare coverage available to those people who qualify for Part A and enrolled in Part B. Typically called Medicare Advantage Plans, Part C provides expanded coverage such as dental, vision, and hearing. There is a fee to enroll in these plans.
- Medicare **Part D**: Prescription drug coverage available to those people who qualify for Part A and are enrolled in Part B. There is a monthly fee associated with this coverage.

- **Fee-for-service plans** allow employees to decide what services they need from any provider; fees are paid by both the employee and the employee's benefits plan through deductibles and coinsurance.
- **Preferred provider organization (PPO) plans** allow insurers to contract with providers of the employees' choosing, with lower fees and better coverage for providers within the organization; fees are paid by deductibles, coinsurance, and co-payments.
- **Health maintenance organization (HMO) plans** emphasize preventative care through fixed costs regardless of the number of visits, but primary care physicians (PCPs) must refer others, and no other providers are covered; fees are paid by deductibles, coinsurance, and co-payments.
- **Point of service (POS) plans** are similar to PPO plans, with certain elements (PCP referrals) of HMO plans; fees are paid by deductibles, coinsurance, and co-payments.
- **Exclusive provider organization (EPO)** is a plan whereby no payments or coverage will be made unless the individual uses a provider within the network of coverage.
- **Consumer-directed health plans** provide tax-favored accounts, such as a flexible spending account (FSA) or a health savings account (HSA), to pay for medical expenses and may allow employees to see any provider of their choosing. However, these plans carry high deductibles and may have low or no coinsurance after the deductible is reached.

Employers usually provide managed care healthcare plans, which are defined as care that ensures an individual receives appropriate and necessary treatment in the most cost-efficient manner possible. There are many forms of healthcare insurance plans, and the increasing cost of insurance has forced employers to absorb additional costs, pass more costs to employees, or find affordable alternatives.

Qualified benefits under these plans might include the following:

- **Medical healthcare coverage**—Plans may include some or all portions of physician services, office visits and exams, prescription drugs, hospital services, maternity services, mental health, physical therapy, and emergency services.
- **Dental coverage**—Plans may include some or all portions of routine exams, cleanings, x-rays, fluoride treatments, orthodontic services, fillings, crowns, and extractions.
- **Dependent care**—Plans may cover some or all portions of on-site childcare, allowances and flexible spending for childcare, daycare information, or flexible scheduling.
- **Short-term disability**—This provides partial income continuation to employees who are unable to work for a short period of time due to an accident or illness. "Short-term" is usually defined as three to six months.
- **Long-term disability**—This provides partial income continuation to employees who are unable to work for long periods of time due to an accident or illness. "Long-term" is usually defined as over six months.
- **Group-term life insurance and accidental death or dismemberment**—This provides financial assistance to an employee or their beneficiaries if the employee has an accident that results in loss of limbs, loss of eyesight, or death. The cost of group plans is frequently lower than individual plans, and payments are based upon the employee's age and annual salary.

Section 125 of the Internal Revenue Code defines a **cafeteria plan** as an employer plan providing participants the opportunity to receive certain benefits on a pretax basis. Funds allocated to these benefits are not included as wages for state or federal income tax purposes and are generally exempt from the Federal Insurance Contributions Act (FICA) and Federal Unemployment Tax Act (FUTA). Unused benefit credits can sometimes be reallocated by the employee to buy more benefits through pretax salary reductions, or the employee may end up losing the unused monies. An employer-sponsored cafeteria plan enables the employee to pick and choose benefits based on their preferences. (This idea of an employee choosing their benefits, like a customer choosing food at a cafeteria, gives cafeteria plans their name; they have nothing to do with actual cafeterias.)

Summarize the purpose of wellness programs.

Describe some of the differences in benefit enrollment terms.

Describe how employers should choose health insurance coverage in benefit programs.

Summarize the aspects of a preferred provider organization (PPO) plan.

Summarize the aspects of a high-deductible health plan (HDHP).

Explain how health savings accounts (HSA) and health reimbursement arrangements (HRA) offset the expense of healthcare coverage for employees.

Employers generally make their benefits packages available to full-time employees; some organizations also extend benefits eligibility to part-time employees.

- Some companies allow employees to enroll in benefits at the very beginning of their employment, while others require employees to work for a period of time, such as 30 or 60 days, before becoming eligible for benefits.
- Employees are able to change their benefits elections each year during annual enrollment, which is also referred to as open enrollment. Annual enrollment usually takes place in the fall, with new benefits elections taking effect on January 1.
- Employees who experience a qualifying event, such as losing eligibility for other coverage, getting married, or becoming a parent, may add or remove coverage or dependents outside of open enrollment.

In addition to providing access to group benefit plans, an employer may cover part or all of the cost of some benefits programs for employees; some companies offset the cost of benefits for dependents as well. Company contributions can add significantly to the value of a company's overall compensation, which is often referred to as total rewards.

Employer-sponsored **wellness programs** are implemented for three primary purposes: (1) to assist employees in improving their health in an effort to prevent serious health problems, (2) to help employers offset the expense of increasing healthcare costs, and (3) to improve employers' overall benefit offerings to remain competitive for attracting and retaining talent. Wellness programs indicate that employers are investing in their employees' health and well-being. Some companies create awareness about the available programs by encouraging employees to participate in a voluntary health assessment or screening as an impetus to encourage healthy lifestyle changes. Employers benefit from these changes through decreased absenteeism, decreased healthcare spending, higher employee morale, and improved productivity. Wellness programs can vary tremendously and may include personalized one-on-one health coaching, nutritional counseling, well-being workshops, healthy snacks at work, stress reduction programs, and fitness activities. Some employers will give monetary incentives to encourage participation in wellness programs.

It has become common practice for employers to offer both a **preferred provider organization (PPO)** plan and a **high-deductible health plan (HDHP)**.

Preferred Provider Organization (PPO)
Higher monthly premiums
Lower deductible
Co-pay applies to office visits and prescriptions (rather than full fee) before deductible has been met
Coinsurance percentage applies after deductible has been met (such as 80% paid by insurance, 20% paid by employee) until out-of-pocket maximum is met
May require using an in-network provider or facility; if out-of-network is allowed, fees will be higher than in-network
Generally best for people whose primary concern is to minimize out-of-pocket expenses for office visits or prescriptions while also having coverage for major medical events.
Cannot be combined with a health savings account.

Health insurance is a very important aspect of a company's benefits package. Employers often pay a portion of employees' health insurance premiums. Some pay the full cost of employee coverage, as well as a portion of the cost for dependent coverage.

Employees don't all have the same needs when it comes to health insurance, so companies often offer multiple plans, with premiums at varying levels. This is to the advantage of the company and its employees alike.

- Employers with 50 or more employees should offer at least one health plan that meets the affordability requirement of the Patient Protection and Affordable Care Act (PPACA) in order to avoid costly penalties.
- Limiting health insurance options to only the plans that meet the affordability requirement of the PPACA would mean that employees wouldn't have access to health plans that offer higher levels of coverage.
- By offering varying levels of coverage at different price points, an employer is providing choices for employees. This helps employees find the right balance between services and cost, letting them get a level of coverage that meets their needs at a price they can pay. It also helps an employer compete for talent with other companies with robust health insurance offerings.

Healthcare options offered by employers have shifted in recent years to a more "consumer-directed" initiative in order for employers to reduce costs and allow employees to choose or customize their healthcare spending. As a result of this shift, employer healthcare options tend to be high-deductible plans. For example, an individual employee could have a deductible of $3,000 and a family deductible of $6,000. This means that the employee must pay the deductible out of pocket before medical insurance begins to pay. This is frequently a burden for employees, so many employers have created and administer programs to help offset the employee expense.

It has become common practice for employers to offer both a **preferred provider organization (PPO)** plan and a **high-deductible health plan (HDHP)**.

High-Deductible Health Plan (HDHP)
Lower monthly premiums
Higher deductible
Individual pays 100% of costs until deductible has been met
Insurance policy pays all covered costs, once the deductible has been met
May require using an in-network provider or facility; if out-of-network is allowed, fees will be higher than in-network
Generally best for healthy people who rarely seek medical care or for those who are likely to reach their deductible very early in the plan year, as the policy covers after that point.
Can be combined with a health savings account.

Discuss eligible medical costs and contribution limits for flexible spending accounts (FSA).

Discuss Health Savings Accounts (HSA).

Discuss Health Reimbursement Arrangements (HRA).

Discuss flexible spending accounts (FSA).

Summarize disability insurance.

Summarize Short-Term Disability (STD) and Long-Term Disability (LTD).

Health Savings Account (HSA)
Requires enrollment in a high-deductible health plan (HDHP)
Can be funded by employer and/or employee
Contribution can be changed at any time
Employee owns the account
Account is portable; it will stay with the employee after separation of employment
Use for qualifying medical expenses
Funds do not expire

Employees are generally eligible to enroll in an HSA, HRA, or FSA when they become eligible for benefits with their employer or during annual enrollment.

Eligible medical care expenses are defined by the IRS and include costs that relate to disease deterrence, diagnosis, or treatment. The costs of procedures undertaken for solely cosmetic reasons are generally not considered expenses for medical care and are not reimbursable. Expenses ineligible under an FSA include procedures and services such as liposuction, Botox treatments, contact lenses, and personal trainers. Eligible expenses do, however, include things like service or guide animals and acupuncture. Employees can also open dependent care FSAs, which allow them to use pretax dollars to pay for dependent care, like daycare.

The IRS determines FSA contribution limits annually. The main drawback to the FSA is that it requires careful budgeting because there is a use-it-or-lose-it provision attached to the benefit. If employees do not use the funds within an account during the given plan year, they may lose the money. Exceptions to this are when the employer opts to offer a grace period, granting an additional 2.5 months to use the funds, or a carryover provision, which is limited to $500. Employers are not required to offer either and can offer only one of the two. They may also offer a run-out period, which gives employees an additional 90 days to make claims for reimbursement.

Flexible Spending Account (FSA)
Does not require participation in a health insurance plan
Can be funded by employee and/or employer
Contribution can be changed at annual enrollment or with a qualifying event
Employer owns the account
Account is not portable; it will not follow the employee after separation of employment
Use for qualifying medical, vision, dental, and dependent care expenses
Funds expire if not used; limited rollover may be possible

Employees are generally eligible to enroll in an HSA, HRA, or FSA when they become eligible for benefits with their employer or during annual enrollment.

Health Reimbursement Account (HRA)
Some HRAs require a health insurance plan; some do not
Funded solely by the employer
Employer sets contribution rules
Employer owns the account
Account is not portable; it will not follow the employee after separation of employment
Use for qualifying medical expenses
Employer sets rules for expiration/rollover

Employees are generally eligible to enroll in an HSA, HRA, or FSA when they become eligible for benefits with their employer or during annual enrollment.

Short-term disability (STD) insurance provides partial income for a short time, usually between three and six months (depending on the policy). Some STD policies provide coverage from the first day of disability, while others have an elimination period of a few weeks.

Long-term disability (LTD) is intended to extend income protection beyond the time covered by a company's STD policy, with the length of coverage varying greatly by policy. Most plans provide coverage for a set number of years; some may last until retirement age. This type of policy usually has an elimination period of at least 90 days, though it can be as long as six months.

Health coverage and healthcare accounts help offset the cost of seeking medical care, but they don't provide income replacement for employees who become unable to work due to illness or injury. That's why short-term disability and long-term disability insurance are often included in employee benefits packages.

Disability insurance policies don't provide full income replacement, but they do provide covered employees with a percentage of their ordinary income for a set period of time when they are unable to work due to illness, injury, or other disability.

In a few states, including (but not limited to) California, New Jersey, and New York, employers are required to provide short-term disability insurance to their employees. Most states don't require employers to provide—or even offer—disability insurance, but it is very common for employers to offer both types of coverage to employees.

Some employers pay for a level of coverage and allow employees to purchase additional protection if they want, while others do not offset the cost of disability insurance. Even in that case, it is usually more affordable for employees to sign up for disability coverage available via their employer than to purchase it on their own, because group plans tend to be less costly than individual coverage.

Explain the purpose of a benefit broker.

List some offerings that benefit brokers commonly supply expertise on.

Describe supplemental benefits and their advantages.

Summarize the purpose and goals of an employee assistance program (EAP).

Describe a gym membership package and its advantages.

Summarize relocation packages.

Generally, benefit brokers supply expertise on some or all of the following common offerings:

- Forms of insurance—Most benefit brokers offer some form of insurance, such as medical, dental, vision, disability, and life.
- Compliance expertise—The broker counsels organizations on benefits to stay in compliance with federal laws, including the Employee Retirement Income Security Act (ERISA), Affordable Care Act (ACA), and specific state and local laws and regulations.
- Overall benefit analysis—This could include cost efficiencies, examination of potential changes based on laws or changing environments, and analysis of existing benefits and related claims.
- Direct employee assistance—This assistance could include direct communication with employees about benefits regarding coverage, claim questions, etc. Additionally, they could provide assistance with enrollment and offer training sessions about benefit options.

Benefit broker fees are usually contingent on the type of coverages and services offered. However, there are others that charge a flat fee based on specific services and offerings.

A **benefit broker** is an external vendor that assists an organization in navigating employee benefit options that are cost-effective and tailored to an organization's needs. Benefit options may include health, dental, vision, financial, and more.

Not all brokers are the same. For example, some might work for a large provider and therefore only offer choices that particular providers offer—think of a large insurance company with only four options for medical insurance to choose from. Others may only specialize in one type of benefit, such as vision. Additionally, some may have a sizable amount of different benefit options in a variety of specialties, but may or may not have extensive knowledge across all benefit offerings.

An **employee assistance program** (EAP) is a program sponsored by an employer that provides confidential counseling services to help employees manage all types of stressful life situations or problems. Because it is sponsored by the employer, an EAP is free to employees. The service is confidential, meaning the employer is not aware of the employee's usage. This confidentiality is primarily due to Health Insurance Portability and Accountability Act (HIPAA) regulations, meaning complete confidentiality is maintained with the third-party vendor contracted to provide the counseling.

An EAP is designed to help the employee, which in turn allows them to be more productive at work. EAP services can vary, but typically include mental health issues, family problems, financial concerns, legal issues, and substance abuse. Usually, the program provides guidance and professional referrals to resources that can help the employee on a short- or long-term basis.

Many companies offer supplemental benefits beyond health and disability coverage. Most companies that offer employee benefits include standard offerings like dental and vision insurance, as well as at least a basic level of life insurance.

Recognizing that offering additional benefits can boost the value of their total rewards package, employers seeking to gain competitive advantage when it comes to recruiting and retaining employees often choose to go above and beyond standard supplemental benefits.

Popular supplemental benefits offerings include the following.

When an employer hires an employee for a job that requires the individual to relocate, the company may offer a relocation assistance program to the employee and their family. Relocation packages vary greatly, but usually include covering the cost of packing up and moving personal belongings and the cost of transporting the employee and their family to where they will be living.

Relocation benefits may also cover additional moving-related costs, such as fees associated with selling a house or breaking a lease, traveling to look for housing prior to the move, temporary housing assistance for a set time at the beginning of the individual's employment, and storage of personal items until a place of residence is secured.

Healthy employees tend to be productive employees who are less at risk for on-the-job injury than others, so it makes sense for a company to offer benefits that help employees get and stay as healthy as possible. That's why gym memberships are such a popular component of employee benefits programs.

Employers often sign up for corporate discount programs with local gyms or nationwide fitness networks, as doing so makes it possible for employees to join at a reduced rate and pay via payroll deduction. Some companies even cover all or part of the cost of gym memberships for employees who opt to participate.

Summarize commuting and traveling benefit packages.

Summarize a retirement plan and its advantages.

Summarize the similarities and differences between 401(k) and 457(b) plans.

List the key aspects of a 401(k) plan.

List the key aspects of a 457(b) plan.

Explain which departments are responsible for payroll.

Retirement plans are an important component of an employee benefits plan. Offering a retirement plan boosts the value of a company's overall compensation plan and helps the organization attract and retain talent. Having access to a workplace retirement plan helps employees save money for retirement via pretax payroll deductions.

Recognizing that commuting and/or parking can be a significant expense for employees, some employers include benefits designed to help offset such costs in their benefits package. Some companies provide commuting stipends or reimbursement for parking expenses, the use of public transportation (such as subways or buses), or rideshare programs.

Additionally, some employers offer special travel/transportation stipends to employees who commute a long distance to work. For example, a company may provide a per diem to employees who drive more than a certain number of miles or who live outside the county where the company is located. This may be based on what county or state the employee drives in from, or the specific number of miles between an employee's home and the worksite.

	401(K)
Employer Type	Private-sector employers
Eligibility	Employees only; must be offered to all employees once they reach 1,000 hours of service
Automatic Enrollment	Permitted
Employee Contributions	Permitted
Employer Contributions	Permitted
Catch-Up Contributions (employees 50+)	Permitted
Written Plan Document	Required
Hardship Withdrawals	Permitted
Pretax contributions	Permitted; taxable upon withdrawal
Post-tax (Roth) contributions	Permitted; not taxable upon withdrawal
Withdraw without penalty	After age $59\frac{1}{2}$

There are a few different types of retirement programs that a company can offer, with 401(k) and 457(b) being among the most common. Only state and local governments and nonprofit organizations can participate in 457(b) plans. Private-sector employers typically offer 401(k) plans. Requirements for 401(k) and 457(b) plans are similar, with a few key differences because 401(k) plans are governed by the Employee Retirement Income Security Act (ERISA) and 457(b) plans are not. Because 401(k) plans fall under ERISA, they are considered qualified plans, while 457(b) plans are considered nonqualified. Both offer tax benefits, with 457(b) plans providing greater flexibility.

In addition to being able to offer 457(b) plans, nonprofit organizations and certain governmental entities can offer 403(b) plans. This type of plan does fall under ERISA and largely mirrors 401(k) plans (except for the types of organizations that can participate).

Payroll is an important function that is usually housed in the HR or accounting department. No matter which of these two departments has the primary responsibility for processing payroll, they have to coordinate. After all, payroll involves critical accounting matters, such as money and tax withholdings/filings, as well as critical HR matters, such as wage and hour compliance, benefits payments, and more.

	457(B)
Employer Type	State and local governments, nonprofit organizations
Eligibility	Open to employees and independent contractors; does not have to be offered to all employees/contractors
Automatic Enrollment	Permitted
Employee Contributions	Permitted
Employer Contributions	Permitted
Catch-Up Contributions (employees 50+)	Permitted
Written Plan Document	Required
Hardship Withdrawals	Permitted
Pretax contributions	Permitted; taxable upon withdrawal
Post-tax (Roth) contributions	Permitted; not taxable upon withdrawal
Withdraw without penalty	Upon leaving employer

Briefly describe the key steps involved in payroll processing.

Explain the primary documents or information needed to process a payroll.

Summarize how a payroll cycle operates.

Discuss how an organization's payroll policy should address the issues of the standard work week, timeclock recordkeeping, and overtime.

Discuss how an organization's payroll policy should address the issues of pay frequency, deductions, and payroll recordkeeping.

Define gross pay and the factors included in it.

There are many documents and information needed to process a payroll. They include but are not limited to the following:

- Completed **W-4** form (for employees)—This form is completed by an employee before or on their first day of work. It documents employee withholding information needed so that the employer can deduct the correct amount of federal income tax from their wages.
- Completed **I-9** form—This form is for employment eligibility verification, and must be completed by an employee's first day of work. It requires showing the employer a combination of identification documents that prove they can legally work in the US.
- **Job application**—This contains consistent, detailed information about an employee such as name, address, education, and dates of employment, which are used to enter information into a payroll system.
- **Bank account information**—This is usually used by an employer to directly deposit an employee's pay into their bank account(s).
- **Medical insurance** form—This form details the amount to be deducted from an employee's pay and their permission for the deduction (usually requires a signature).
- **Retirement plan** form—This form details the amount being deducted for various retirement plan options. As with medical insurance, an employee signature is required for an employer to deduct from an employee's pay.

Payroll processing is a system that an employer utilizes to manage the payment of wages to its employees. Payroll processing is more than just issuing a paycheck. There are other components that need to be addressed, such as legal compliance with all federal, state, and local laws and regulations, including reporting requirements; the time period for record retention of information; and all aspects of control and security. Generally, the major steps involved in payroll processing include gathering the time worked per employee for a designated time period, calculating and applying cost of benefits and deductions, distributing paychecks (direct deposit or paper check), and following retention procedures. The employer must then file and remit payroll taxes. An organization can face expensive penalties if payroll taxes are not accurate and on time. Most organizations use payroll software or outsource to a third-party payroll processing service.

A payroll policy is a set of guidelines and protocols established to ensure that payroll is accurate, processed on time, and conducted with strict adherence to all payroll laws and regulations.

- To comply with the Fair Labor Standards Act (FLSA), a **standard work week** needs to be defined and usually constitutes seven consecutive 24-hour periods. A work week doesn't have to start on Monday, but can begin on any day of the week.
- There should be a system in place, electronic or paper, to **accurately record employee hours** worked, with an approval process to verify the information is correct. State laws and regulations may require employers to give breaks from work for rest, meals, etc., after a given number of hours worked. These breaks also need to be reflected in total hours worked.

A **payroll cycle** or schedule refers to the frequency that an employer issues pay to an employee. The most common cycle is biweekly, or every other week, for a total of 26 paychecks per year. However, an organization could also offer a weekly cycle, meaning 52 paychecks a year; or possibly a monthly cycle, with 12 paychecks a year; etc. An organization can choose their payroll schedule as long as it is in compliance with all federal, state, and local laws and regulations. Many states require employers to pay their employees biweekly, others have more specific requirements, and some have no specified schedules. However, an organization must also consider what the employees would prefer. Most employees prefer to get paid more frequently as compared to less frequently, especially those employees earning low wages. Employers must also weigh the cost of processing payroll more frequently, because it will cost more. An organization must decide and communicate a consistent payroll schedule.

Payroll starts with gross pay, which is the total amount an employee has earned during the pay period. This includes salary for exempt employees, as well as straight-time and overtime earnings for nonexempt employees. Gross pay must include base pay and additional pay owed to employees, such as shift differentials for working a challenging shift or hazardous assignment, as well as other compensation such as incentive compensation or bonuses.

A payroll policy is a set of guidelines and protocols established to ensure that payroll is accurate, processed on time, and conducted with strict adherence to all payroll laws and regulations.

- **How often employees are paid** should be detailed—whether biweekly, weekly, monthly, etc.—and what days they will receive their pay.
- A **payroll policy** should also explain deductions: mandatory deductions, such as Social Security and other taxes, and voluntary deductions, like health insurance and retirement plans. In addition, it should give further explanation of pre- and post-tax information. All the different wage structures should be explained, such as hourly pay, salary, bonuses, commission, and stock options.
- Finally, all time periods for **payroll recordkeeping** should be documented, as well as applicable security measures.

List the steps involved in processing payroll.

Explain payroll processing.

Describe mandatory deductions that may be included when processing payroll.

Describe voluntary deductions that may be included when processing payroll.

Summarize wage statements and the information included on them.

Explain what paid time off (PTO) from work means.

Processing payroll involves making sure that deductions are properly withheld from each employee's paycheck. This involves a lot more than just making sure that an employee's tax deductions are correct. Employees may pay for a number of items via payroll deduction, including voluntary deductions for employee benefits, mandatory deductions such as income tax, and—in some cases—other financial obligations.

When processing payroll, it's very important to properly deduct taxes from each employee's compensation, including federal income tax; Federal Insurance Contributions Act (FICA) tax, which funds Social Security and Medicare; and any applicable state or local taxes that an employer is required to withhold. Tax withholdings must be paid to appropriate government agencies, and appropriate paperwork must be submitted in the required timeframe (which varies based on the type of tax and agency).

An employer must also keep track of, properly file, and report company-paid taxes. For example, the company makes FICA contributions in addition to what employees themselves pay. The employer also has to pay Federal Unemployment Tax Act (FUTA) and state unemployment insurance (SUI) premiums.

The most common voluntary deductions include benefits premiums paid by the employee; contributions to a health savings account (HSA), health reimbursement account (HRA), and/or flexible spending account (FSA); and contributions to an employer-sponsored retirement plan. Employees may authorize other voluntary deductions, such as:

- Contributions to a charitable organization
- Payment for on-site parking at the workplace
- Gym membership fees as part of a corporate membership
- Other programs for which the company allows payroll deduction

In addition to payroll taxes, mandatory deductions may include things like court-ordered child support or alimony, as well as wage garnishments for unpaid debts, payments ordered due to bankruptcy, or unpaid income tax. An employer is obligated to withhold mandatory deductions and submit the funds to the organization or agency specified on the court order or judgment received. Most states allow employers to charge employees a small fee (generally between \$1 and \$5) for each garnishment, to offset the administrative burden of processing them. This fee would also be withheld as a deduction.

Employees will need to take time off from work to attend to various life circumstances and events. There is no simple formula for an organization to follow when developing guidelines for PTO. PTO varies tremendously from one organization to another, and much depends on the needs of the business as well as what employees need. Furthermore, PTO must comply with all federal, state, and local laws and regulations. Some organizations, like the federal government, have rigid guidelines; others have looser, almost employee-determined PTO days. For instance, some companies might give employees 12 vacation days, 6 sick days, 3 bereavement days, and 10 holidays, then let the employee choose and categorize their PTO days. A PTO policy usually states the guidelines and processes for an employee to request PTO and obtain necessary approvals.

Wage statements also include information about employee leave, including how much paid time off (PTO), vacation time, or sick leave an employee currently has available to use, and how much (if any) of each type of leave the employee used during the current pay period. Wage statements may also show how much leave an employee has used so far in the current year.

An employer may also show other types of leave on wage statements, including Family and Medical Leave (FML) or leaves of absence for personal or other reasons. Reporting leave on wage statements helps employees know where they stand in terms of their accrued leave at any given time.

List and explain some examples of paid time off (PTO).

Explain unpaid leave and provide some examples.

Describe a final paycheck and the regulations surrounding it.

Summarize what information is included in a total rewards statement (TRS).

Define a vision statement.

Define a mission statement.

Unpaid leave is time off from work that is approved by the employer, but not compensated in any way. There are many reasons an employee may need to take unpaid leave. Every employee request and situation must be carefully considered by an employer to make sure it is consistent with organizational policy and legally compliant with all federal, state, and local laws and regulations. If an employee is requesting unpaid leave under the parameters of the Family and Medical Leave Act (FMLA), then the employee's unpaid leave is mandatory, and the employee is guaranteed to keep their job and benefits upon returning to work. An unpaid leave of absence can also occur when an employee has used up all of their paid time off. Assuming the request does not have to be granted under federal, state, or local laws and regulations, it is up to the employer's discretion and policies.

In some instances, the employer can also force an employee to take unpaid leave if the workplace does not have enough work, a practice sometimes referred to as a **furlough**. During a furlough, employees typically have access to benefits. Furloughs are sometimes implemented to avoid a staff reduction such as layoffs. Another example of when employees could be furloughed is when coming to work is temporarily unsafe, like during a national pandemic. Paying or not paying employees during such a furlough is up to the employer's discretion and is dependent on many other factors.

There are many categories for PTO. The following are some common examples:
- **Personal** time—Time off to attend to various life activities.
- **Sick** time—Time off for personal illness, injury, or general medical care. Sick time may also be covered under the Family and Medical Leave Act, ADA, short- and long-term disability, or workers' compensation.
- **Vacation** time—Time off from work for recreation or fun.
- **Holidays**—Time off to celebrate recognized holidays.
- **Floating holidays**—Time off to celebrate holidays that might not be recognized by the organization.
- **Bereavement**—Time off due to a death in the employee's immediate family. Some organizations even have bereavement PTO days for the death of a pet.
- **Jury duty**—Time off from work for compulsory jury duty.
- **Compensatory (comp)** time—Credited time off from work for eligible employees who would prefer time off instead of payment. Not all employees are eligible for comp time because FLSA mandates that all nonexempt workers must be compensated for time worked, both standard and overtime.
- **Maternity and paternity** leave—Time off following the birth or adoption of a child.
- **Military** leave Time off for military service obligations. Includes the US Armed Forces, the National Guard, and state defense forces. The Uniformed Services Employment and Reemployment Rights Act (USERRA) provides certain job protections, and employers also frequently offer a supplement to offset the difference between regular pay and military pay.

A total rewards statement is a document that shows the full value of an employee's compensation, which is usually much higher than the actual wages or salary paid to an employee. Employers are not required to produce this kind of statement, but it is considered best practice to periodically provide each employee with an individualized total rewards statement. Many organizations provide employees with a total rewards statement annually; some do so quarterly or even monthly.

Why should an employer consider producing yet another statement to share with employees? Because employees tend to think about their pay solely in terms of their hourly rate of pay or their monthly or annual salary. However, that's only part of the true value of their compensation. A total rewards statement shows the full value, including what the employer pays above and beyond the rate of pay, such as employer benefits contributions, FICA payments (employees pay half; employers pay half), unemployment insurance, retirement plan contributions, and more.

When employees see all of this summed up in a single statement, this helps to clarify the full value of their total rewards package above and beyond their pay rate. Having this information can contribute positively to employee satisfaction and retention. After all, the more that employees know about the full picture of their compensation, the less likely they are to consider leaving their current employer for a small difference in pay; at least, they should know the full picture of how another employer's offer compares with the total value of their current position. Often, a marginally higher pay rate is worth less when other factors are taken into consideration.

The final paycheck for an employee who is exiting the company should include all compensation owed to that employee, including their final salary or wages, any commissions or incentives owed to them, and the payout for any accrued paid leave due to them per company policy.

Regulations regarding final pay vary by state. In some states, the final paycheck can be issued with the next regular payroll cycle, such that the employee receives the check at the same time they would have gotten it if they were continuing to work for the company. However, in some places, an employee must be given their final paycheck on the last day they work for the company.

A **mission statement** describes an organization's purpose and the activities an organization will pursue to achieve its vision. This declaration is designed to offer three basic elements: (1) an overall description of who the company is, (2) a description of what the company does, and (3) an explanation of why the company exists. The statement also serves as a communication tool explaining, at a high level, how an organization will achieve its goals with its customers, its employees, and all other stakeholders. A mission statement also explains to suppliers, customers, and clients why they should want to do business with an organization. In fact, organizations frequently use their mission statement theme in advertising and marketing collateral. A mission statement could also be thought of as the guiding force of an organization's operating manual, helping employees and other stakeholders better understand its central purpose. A mission statement might be altered over time as an organization grows and evolves.

A **vision statement** provides a concise assertion that captures what the leadership team foresees as the future of the organization. This long-term, result-driven declaration serves as a guiding, inspirational force for the organization. A vision statement is aspirational and usually contains several of the following key elements: it is inspirational, it is future-oriented, it captures the organization's culture, and it strives to articulate its benefits in the future. Here are a few examples of notable organizations and their vision statements:
- Disney—"To make people happy."
- Ben & Jerry's—"Making the best ice cream in the nicest possible way."
- Apple—"We believe that we are on the face of the earth to make great products and that's not changing."
- TED—"Spread ideas."

A vision statement is vital for the planning and execution of organizational strategies. As an organization grows and evolves, a vision statement might be altered over time.

List the key differences between a vision and mission statement.

Define organizational values.

Summarize the purpose of organizational culture.

Explain the connection between strong organizational culture and success.

Summarize why HR is sometimes called the "caretaker" of organizational culture.

Explain how culture is frequently unwritten.

Values are part of an organization's strategic plan and define what is important to a particular business. Organizational values are frequently referred to as the "heart" of the organization, helping form the culture and playing a significant role in directing employee behavior. Some organizations choose to document their values and include them with their vision and mission statements. In other organizations, values are more informal and/or unwritten. Organizational values help drive decision making in the organization and ultimately signify what it stands for. These values serve as a filter, defining how organizational tasks should be accomplished. When organizational values and employee behavior are not in sync, conflict can develop, causing negative consequences and possibly interfering with the achievement of strategic goals. Values should be understood by all employees and serve to enhance employee contributions and commitment to the organization.

A vision statement and mission statement are essential components of an organization's strategic planning process. They both help the organization directionally prepare for the future and achieve its goals. However, a mission statement highlights what the organization is currently doing, while a vision statement highlights what the organization strives to achieve in the future. As such, a mission statement is more short-term, usually one to three years, detailing the organization's purpose and current activities. A vision statement, on the other hand, is a long-term declaration that is more inspirational, highlighting the organization's hope for the future. Additionally, a vision statement is directional and may or may not be crystal-clear about what the future state will look like. In contrast, a mission statement is crystal-clear in its goals, objectives, and desired performance for successful achievement. A vision statement can only be achieved if the mission statement is successfully implemented.

In order to sustain a strong culture, an organization's values and beliefs must be shared and adhered to by every employee. Maintaining a strong sense of culture can lead to enhanced collaboration among employees and more efficient decision making, and can ultimately drive competitive advantage—all of which contribute to making an organization successful. In other words, behavior is supported or justified by the common denominator of a culture developed by organizational leaders and driven by leaders and employees into all aspects of work. All members in an organization have the framework of culture to guide their behavior and act as an informal control system. Often, an ineffective culture can lead to employee disengagement, high employee turnover, poor customer relationships, and loss of revenue and business. For some enterprises, culture has been a significant factor in their ability to implement strategies and successfully execute the mission statement.

Organizational culture is the way activities are accomplished. It is a tone set by leaders for everyone in the organization to share basic beliefs that support an overall direction and strategy. Employees play a pivotal role in achieving organizational goals by behaving in a certain way, knowing they will be rewarded for displaying the organization's values. Organizational culture is the foundation that drives how an organization operates. It is often referred to as the force behind an organization's mission attainment and success. There is no specific model or formula to develop a culture. A robust culture is grounded in shared beliefs and common goals and is supported by strategies and processes in an organization. However, it is often challenging to define an organization's specific culture. Some keywords that might capture an organization's culture include: family-oriented, innovative, customer-focused, motivating, fast-paced, rewarding, ethical, fun, technology-driven, inclusive.

Mission and vision statements are literally documented with specific words. However, an organization's culture is about behavior and what is observed, heard, and felt—in other words, it is unwritten. Culture is about the degree to which an organization subscribes to or pursues its mission, be it aggressively or slow and steady; about the value placed on people and their work-life balance; or about the hierarchy of the organizational structure. Some unwritten cultural cues could include dress code, size or location of offices, open doors, hallway or breakroom conversations, friendliness, laughter, or facial expressions. Unwritten rules are simply the way an organization operates, and are deep-rooted in its culture. Other unwritten rules are operational and can easily be learned by observation. For example, in some organizations, employees feel it is in their best interest to always agree with the organization's leaders or else possibly face negative consequences. Other organizations may encourage open and honest feedback with company leaders and reward new or alternative ideas. Employees usually learn to adapt and alter their behavior based on observations.

One of the most important assets of an organization is its people. HR plays an essential role in ensuring that an organization's culture is built and cultivated in order to gain or maintain a competitive advantage. HR must work with leaders not only to understand strategic direction and monetary goals, but also to influence leaders by showing them how an organization's culture can drive the achievement of these priorities. HR can influence this by doing the following:

- Communicating and reinforcing an organization's values
- Building and maintaining communication and continuous feedback
- Ensuring ethical standards are defined, understood, and practiced
- Providing professional development and training
- Defining roles and responsibilities for employees
- Developing and maintaining a recognition and/or rewards system
- Observing and recognizing organizational and specific employee relations problems, and facilitating solutions
- Motivating employees in order to maintain job satisfaction
- Establishing external professional relationships that benefit the organization

Define the connection between tradition and organizational culture.

Describe the importance of mission, vision, and values statements.

Explain the purpose of a human resource information system (HRIS).

Describe the main functions of a human resource information system.

Describe several benefits of a human resource information system (HRIS).

Describe several benefits of a human resource information system (HRIS).

The mission/vision/values statements of an organization serve many purposes, but primarily they serve as the heart of the organization and its guiding principles. If an organization is dedicated to equity and diversity, those elements will be present in all aspects of the workplace, from hiring to advertising to sourcing. Equity and diversity would not exist merely as enrichment programs or feel-good declarations. These statements would define what the organization stands for and how people within that organization are expected to behave. When organizational behavior embodies the statements listed in the values, vision, or mission, the influence on the company culture is undeniable. Employees feel as though the organization has followed through, and it stands for what it says. There truly is support and buy-in from the top down. These principles help individuals, teams, and departments to collaborate to meet a common purpose, facilitating a culture of support and teamwork. When the workforce is aligned with and inspired by these principles, it can lead to greater employee engagement and motivation toward achieving goals and objectives. These statements influence how employees feel about the organization, and how they communicate about the organization to others.

When a company fails to live by the guiding principles, it sends a poor message to the work base that the organization cannot be trusted and does not believe in its own message. Employees may wonder why they must abide by the statements when they don't see others doing the same. This can negatively influence the company culture and create a toxic workplace where unethical and immoral behaviors, actions, and attitudes can flourish.

Usually, an organization's culture is based on factors that contributed to its success in the past, and thus became tradition. In its early stages, an organization's leaders play a significant role in establishing its culture, thereby planting the seeds of behavioral norms that are closely aligned with their values. These norms will blossom and grow over time to become tradition, shaping an organization's culture. Tradition, when embedded in an organization's culture, can take many forms. How conflicts are resolved—whether respectfully, quietly, privately, or perhaps in the open with raised voices—serves as an example of culture. Decision making is another example; one organization might make all decisions in a hierarchical manner, while another organization might have a more ad hoc decision-making process. "Culture" is an all-encompassing term that includes beliefs and an organization's traditions that are passed down over time. HR should be aware of an organization's traditions and their positive or negative impacts on the organization.

Some HRIS functions could include the following:

- **Tracking basic employee information**—May include name, address, salary, and emergency contact information.
- **Keeping company documentation**—May include items such as employee handbooks, emergency procedures, and safety guidelines.
- **Benefit administration**—Could include enrollment capabilities, insurance changes, attendance and time off, and the ability for employees to look up and track information.
- **Payroll integration**—Reduces duplication of efforts with payroll and increases efficiencies.
- **Applicant tracking**—Allows recruiters to manage an applicant's information, then move the applicant to employee status and retain information.
- **Performance management**—Could include performance evaluations; possible improvement plans can follow the employee throughout the organization.
- **Tracking disciplinary issues**—May include the recording of demotions, suspensions, or other negative actions taken, all of which may be important to retain even after an employee leaves the organization.
- **Training**—Retains records of required certifications, licenses, and/or other compliance training.

A **human resource information system** (HRIS) is a computer system designed to help HR professionals carry out the day-to-day HR functions necessary for an organization to continue functioning normally. Most HRISs are designed to collect and store data related to the use of employee benefits, hiring, placement, training and evaluations of employees, payroll, and information about the work performed by employees during a given period of time. An HRIS is designed to help an HR professional carry out all primary functions associated with HR needs, which include benefits administration, payroll, time and labor management, and human resources management. An HRIS not only aids the HR department, but also helps the entire organization function effectively.

- **Training management**—An HRIS may store relevant training information for an organization. Employees, depending on their occupation or position, may be required to have current training credentials; training may be legally required; or training may enhance an employee's skill set, thereby increasing an organization's competitive advantage.
- **Communication**—Some HRIS software enables an organization to quickly distribute information or changes to everyone, or segments of a population. This communication could include procedural changes, handbook updates, weather-related closings, warnings, and policies. Some HRIS programs are even designed to distribute and analyze surveys.
- **Self-service**—Some HRIS programs have the capability to respond to employee questions about things like benefits, time off, and policies, thereby reducing the amount of time HR professionals spend answering simple questions.
- **E-signature capabilities**—As information and communication have become more digitized, so has the need for electronic signatures (e-signatures) on contracts, forms, etc. Many HRIS products have a feature whereby an electronic signature can be stored, which reduces a tremendous amount of paperwork.

There are many benefits afforded by an HRIS:

- **Productivity**—The primary purpose of an HRIS is to improve HR productivity. An HRIS enables HR to quickly access information, thereby increasing the speed of decision making.
- **Reduced errors**—Whenever the manipulation of data occurs, the opportunity for error can increase, which in HR could lead to financial loss, unwanted legal issues, and/or possible damage to the brand or image.
- **Metric analysis**—Analyzing employee-related metrics such as recruiting costs, attendance, and benefit usage is an essential HR function. An HRIS allows for the proper storage and retrieval of needed data for calculations and statistical analysis impacting the organization.
- **Attendance management**—Tracking employee time off, whether for illness, PTO, or vacation, reduces the need for HR to manually capture and track all time-off situations.
- **Payroll management**—Capturing payroll-related information, such as time off or certain benefit selections, makes it easier to keep accurate records and expediently retrieve information for analysis.
- **Benefit administration**—Keeping records of health insurance, pension information, bonuses, and any other benefits enables HR to not only quickly retrieve data, but also efficiently analyze trends.

Summarize the disadvantages of a human resource information system (HRIS).

Summarize how HR might use predictive analytics.

Summarize why communication is critical in the workplace.

Define upward, downward, and lateral communication flows.

Define diagonal and external communication flows.

List some main channels of communication and when they should be used.

Predictive analytics is a type of technology that uses reliable current or historical data to forecast future behavior. These analytics technologically apply the old adage that "past behavior is the best indicator of future behavior." However, predictive analytics uses science and technology to make predictions that are usually very specific. Predictive analytics uses many different statistical techniques that scrutinize reliable current or historical data and related outcomes. The goal is to generate a formula or algorithm that best replicates the outcomes. This information can then be leveraged to forecast reliable future outcomes.

HR captures a tremendous amount of data about employees, and the data is usually stored in its HRIS. This data could be used to generate predictive models for HR professionals to enable better organizational decision making instead of relying on an unquantifiable feeling or some other non-science-based metric. HR analytics is being used more frequently to help an organization predict and respond to a variety of people policies. Some of the areas to which predictive analytics is being applied include improving employee turnover, predicting revenue through employee engagement measures, improving hiring decisions, and evaluating employment risk.

The purpose of an HRIS is to safely store employee-related information, retrieve it efficiently, and analyze the data, allowing for more expedient organizational decision making. In other words, it is a system that is used to enhance the quality and efficiencies of management's decision making. Sometimes these advantages come at a cost and could become a disadvantage. The following are some of the possible disadvantages of an HRIS:

- **Human error**—There is an old adage: "Garbage in, garbage out." If a human error is made in data input, then there will be an error in the output, putting the organization at risk of making a decision based on false information.
- **Expense**—An HRIS can be costly to purchase, maintain, and update. Also, depending on the system, it could require an organization to hire an HRIS specialist to efficiently administer and maintain it. Additionally, new systems and updates require training. The time spent on training needs to show a positive return on investment for the HRIS to be cost effective.
- **Technical malfunctions**—System downtime can occur, which takes time and effort to resolve, possibly costing the organization time and money.
- **Unauthorized access**—As with any technology system, necessary precautions such as encryption and firewalls need to be taken so that only those with a "need to know" have access to HRIS information.

Organizational communication flows follow five main paths. Those paths are downward, upward, lateral, diagonal, and external.

- *Downward* communication flow occurs when communication travels from a higher level within the organization to a lower level. This type of communication takes place when leaders communicate to direct reports. Downward communication is made up of work-related information that employees need in order to understand expectations and complete tasks. Examples include providing feedback on performance, communicating the organizational mission and vision to employees, and detailing job instructions.
- *Upward* communication flow occurs when communication flows through to a higher level. Direct reports use upward communication to address issues, report problems, and ask questions of leaders. Upward communication can also be used to foster a collaborative decision-making process. Open expression and dialogue regarding ideas, opinions, feelings, and views can also be facilitated through upward communication. Pulse surveys, satisfaction surveys, and suggestion boxes are all ways to facilitate upward communication.
- *Lateral* communication flow occurs when communication is exchanged at the same hierarchical level within the organization. This type of communication takes place when peers or same-level leaders communicate with one another. This can foster cooperation between team members, share information, resolve conflicts, and solve problems. It can help build teams and develop relationships. Lateral communication is also important in providing emotional and social support and assistance within the workplace.

Workplace communication is the exchange of information and ideas in an organization. Good workplace communication is necessary in order to have a high-performing organizational culture and operate with maximum efficiency. The most important aspect of communication is not simply saying or technically communicating information, but rather ensuring that the information is received accurately and is correctly understood by the intended audience. Effective communication is critical in order for an organization to achieve its goals. The goal of effective workplace communication is to avoid confusion or ambiguity, build collaboration among employees, shape a positive culture, and create accountability. Frequently, the best measure of effective communication is to observe what works and what doesn't work. Additionally, workplace communication is a strong mechanism for all members of an organization to provide input and come away feeling that their thoughts were heard and valued.

Communication can be transmitted through a wide variety of channels or media, such as phone, email, face to face, reports, presentations, or social media. The chosen method should fit both the audience and the type of communication. **Information-rich communication channels** include phone, videoconferencing, and face-to-face meetings or presentations. **Information-lean communication channels** include email, fliers, newsletters, and reports. When trying to sell a product or service, a salesman might use a series of phone calls, face-to-face meetings, and presentations. This is because information-rich media are more interactive, which is more appropriate for complex messages that may need clarification. Rich and verbal communications should be used when there is time urgency, immediate feedback is required, ideas can be simplified with explanations, or emotions may be affected. Lean and written communications should be used when the communicator is simply stating facts or needs information permanently recorded.

Organizational communication flows follow five main paths. Those paths are downward, upward, lateral, diagonal, and external.

- *Diagonal* communication flow occurs when managers or leads communicate with employees from other departments or workgroups. This takes place often when working on projects, initiatives, or training, to ensure each area is accurately included and represented. When utilized effectively, diagonal communication can help eliminate misunderstandings and promote a culture of open dialogue.
- *External* communication flow is communication between leaders and external groups like suppliers, vendors, and service providers. This occurs when seeking new products or services, negotiating contracts, or ordering materials and supplies. External communication is critical to ensure that an organization has the materials and items needed to function successfully.

Describe the importance of oral communication in the workplace.

Explain the usage and applications of using email, text, or instant messaging (IM) as a form of communication.

Discuss the key characteristics and differences between passive and aggressive communication styles.

Describe the passive-aggressive communication style.

Explain what it means to have an assertive communication style.

Describe how to deliver clear messages.

Emailing, texting, and instant messaging (IM) are increasingly popular forms of workplace communication because they are simple and efficient. The workplace is becoming more technology-driven, and many companies have implemented written communication policies that dictate what types of workplace communication are allowed via text and email versus phone and face-to-face. These policies vary by company, but they frequently outline or offer guidelines as to which form of communication is appropriate situationally. In general, email, texting, and IM are excellent forms of communication for information that is clear, brief, and actionable. Examples include asking a coworker if they can attend a meeting at a particular date and time, requesting someone to review information and respond, or asking for specific information. When writing via any form of technological communication, one must consider whether the communication is necessary and if it is appropriate. For instance, a phone call might be more efficient if there is going to be a lot of dialogue. Additionally, email, texting, IM, or really any form of writing might not be appropriate if sensitive or bad news needs to be communicated, because it can be challenging to communicate compassion, empathy, and tone. Information shared in this format could be misinterpreted, causing further harm. Similarly, anything put in an email, text, or IM could inadvertently be shared, potentially causing harm or embarrassment.

A **passive-aggressive communication** style is challenging to describe, but easy to recognize. While the passive-aggressive communicator doesn't literally state their feelings of anger, disagreement, or dissatisfaction, they will communicate their true thoughts in subtle ways. This communication style is covert because the passive-aggressive person desires to suggest their discontent without overtly stating that they are upset or disagree about something.

Examples of this communication style in the workplace might include blaming others for personal issues or problems, starting rumors or gossip to distract or undermine leadership, facially expressing their opinion instead of using words, being quick to embarrass others, perhaps using words like "whatever" or sarcastically saying "fine," or verbally agreeing to something with no intention of doing whatever was agreed to. Frequently the goal of a passive-aggressive communicator is to cause others to convey the feelings that the passive-aggressive person is feeling. This gives the passive-aggressive person the satisfaction of exerting their power over someone else.

Delivering messages can be difficult, especially if the context is serious. The message content should be tailored to fit the audience. This requires understanding the roles, expectations, and perspective of recipients. First, focus on eliminating any barriers or vague wording that may interfere with interpreting the message. Once the proper channel for delivery is selected, it may be important to focus on nonverbal signals and ensure that they coincide with the mood of the message content. Finally, messages should allow for feedback that will lead to follow-up discussions. If a message is complex, such as a business change or new benefits offering, it may be critical to share repeated reminders and have open lines of communication to reduce confusion and ensure success.

Oral communication is the art of using speech to deliver information about ideas, feelings, and opinions. Good communication skills are not only a necessity in personal life, but extremely important in the workplace. In fact, most job offers require or at least prefer applicants with "excellent written and oral communication skills." Oral communication is how relationships and trust are formed among employees. Poor oral communication can lead to misunderstandings and conflict, and results in a loss of workplace productivity.

Oral communication is a combination of which words a person chooses to use and how those words are communicated. The marriage of what and how a person communicates while speaking allows for the smooth flow of communication among employees and a more productive work environment. Additionally, this marriage of "what and how" is significant in HR because critical information is frequently communicated by speaking, as with job offers, performance improvement, compensation changes, and layoffs. Usually, for information that is more emotional in nature, oral communication is the preferred method, although sometimes the same information is contained in a written follow-up. The right words, tone, and speed of oral communication impact how something is understood. Another critical component of good oral communication is active listening, as the workplace is more successful if opinions are heard and employees feel engaged.

Communication styles vary by individual, and there is not one communication style that is correct because so much depends on the situation and individual preference. Someone with a **passive communication** style frequently acts indifferent, may not express their feelings, and prefers to listen to others as opposed to objecting or disagreeing. A passive communicator usually wants to avoid causing any conflict, even to the point of remaining silent when they should speak out. In fact, sometimes their silence causes a misunderstanding. In the workplace, a person with this style of easygoing, patient communication can be effective at calming nerves and putting others before themselves. They almost never complain and rarely object to work.

By contrast, someone with an **aggressive communication** style has no problem voicing their opinion at every opportunity, and frequently is rude and hurtful when speaking. The key for an aggressive communicator is to get their opinion heard and listened to, no matter the consequences. "I'm right, you're wrong" could be the motto of an aggressive communicator. They put their needs ahead of others. Despite these often-unwanted characteristics, aggressive communicators who can temper or control their more negative tendencies often make excellent leaders because of their ability to attract attention and convince others to follow them.

An **assertive communication** style is defined by honest, direct verbalization about one's thoughts or opinions without judging others for their beliefs. The premise of an assertive communicator is to communicate in a polite manner while demonstrating respect for one's own beliefs or ideas as well as the opinions of others. When others deal with an assertive communicator, they feel comfortable and welcome to express their feelings because they know civility and consideration for all is an objective that will be met.

An assertive communicator will try to find a solution that benefits all parties, allowing everyone to benefit or at least letting them feel as though their opinion was heard and valued. For example, an assertive communicator might respond with, "I really think this is the way to proceed, but I'm genuinely open to hearing your opinion." Those with an assertive communication style frequently use "I" statements when conversing. An "I" statement allows someone to be assertive without putting the listener on the defensive. It permits communicators to take ownership of their feelings without implying they are the cause of the problem. For example, instead of saying, "You never listen to me and probably aren't listening now," one could say, "I feel my concerns are not being heard." In the workplace, an assertive communicator is excellent at building and maintaining productive teams and collaboratively solving conflict.

Describe key characteristics of an active listener.

Explain the importance and creation of an organization's reporting structure.

Describe the key elements of a flat organizational structure.

Describe the key elements of a hierarchical organizational structure.

Hierarchy Structure

Explain the key elements of a divisional structure.

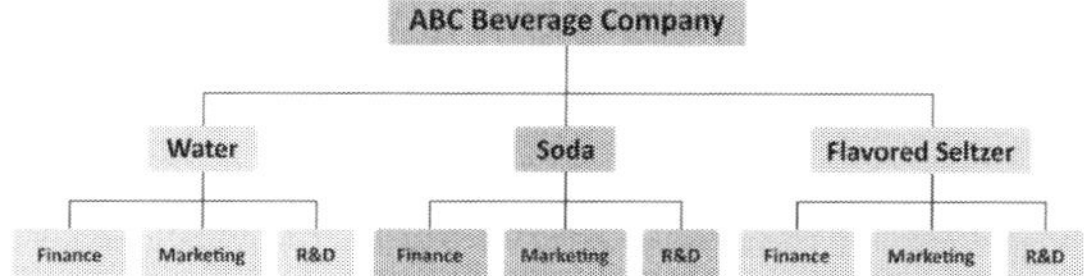

Divisional Organization Chart

Describe the matrix organizational structure.

Matrix Organization Chart

Organizational structure allows organizations to carry out their goals in the most efficient and productive manner possible. Basically, organizational structure is the way work flows through an organization. There is no such thing as a one-size-fits-all organizational structure; it is dependent on what work needs to be accomplished, and by whom. Organizational structure can be formal or less formal as well as flexible depending on the organizational goals. Typically, organizational structure is aligned with the organization's strategy.

Interdependencies between business functions and output need to be carefully examined. This requires looking closely at the relationship among the following: leadership, which is responsible for strategy and results; the organization, which determines how processes and operations strategy are implemented; the jobs and the responsibilities needed to perform key organizational roles; and the people whose experience is needed to execute operations and achieve strategic goals. Understanding and maintaining the sync between these interdependencies is what drives the type of organizational structure that will work best for a business.

The creation of an organization reporting structure is based on several factors:
- Job departmentalization—How jobs are grouped together to complete work
- Span of control—Number of people who report to a supervisor or manager
- Centralization—Decision making that is conducted by upper-level management
- Decentralization—Decision making that is conducted by lower- or middle-level management

Active listening is an important component of communication that requires paying close attention to what is being said. It often involves making eye contact and appropriately nodding to show engagement. To gain a better understanding, listeners should try to understand things from the speaker's point of view, or visualize what they are saying. It is important to be considerate, avoid distractions or interruptions, and respond appropriately. Additionally, listeners should try to pick up on emotional cues beyond the literal words that are used. Even if the message differs from the active listener's own opinion, the listener will try to focus on accepting what the other person has to say rather than being critical. Active listeners should make sure to fully hear what the other person is saying before formulating their own response. When compared to passive listeners, active listeners are more connected and conscientious.

A **hierarchy organization chart** looks like a tall pyramid and is sometimes called a functional or functional hierarchical organizational chart. The top portion of the chart is almost always a single person, usually the president or CEO. The chart widens slightly on the second level with employees who report directly to the leader, possibly vice presidents. It widens further at the next level for employees who report to vice presidents, possibly directors. This pattern continues, with the chart widening as it includes more employees, until it reaches the bottom level with the lowest title designations. Each level is subordinate to the levels above it.

This organization structure is best suited for large organizations, in which supervision and responsibility are clearly established. Typically, the hierarchical environment utilizes specialists or positions with expertise in a specific area that tend to have a strong allegiance to their area or department within the business. This quality can be good for the individual department, but it makes horizontal communication across the other areas of the business very challenging, especially when decision making may be a benefit for one department and not necessarily for another. Sometimes a hierarchical structure is considered very bureaucratic, thereby possibly causing a slow response to changing market conditions or customer needs, and making the entire structure generally less flexible.

A **flat organizational structure** can be represented as a list of company employees, usually managers and supervisors, who report to a single leader. It is sometimes called a horizontal organizational structure because the list is usually arranged horizontally along a single line below the leader. This type of organization chart is most often used by small or startup companies. Also typical of this structure is that middle management is eliminated, thereby allowing employees to more easily make independent decisions and change direction quickly. This structure also provides employees with more responsibility, which increases employee involvement and leads to a freer exchange of ideas and communication. However, this type of structure can also make it challenging for employees because supervision is sometimes not so clear. Overall, a flat organizational structure is very difficult to maintain as a company grows larger.

Flat (Horizontal) Organization Chart

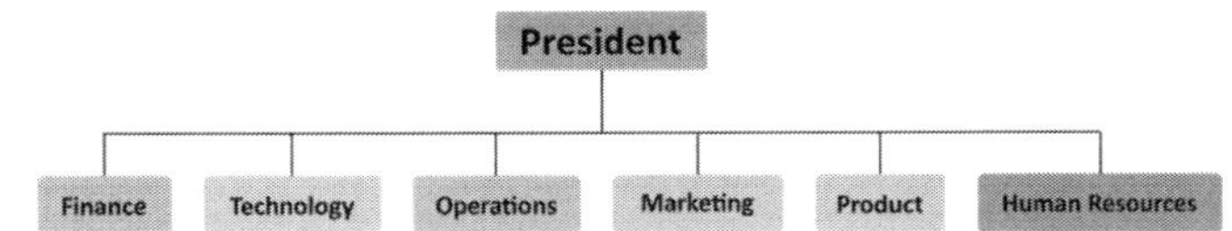

The **matrix organizational structure** is the combination of the flat structure and the divisional structure. Basically, employees are supervised by at least two managers, who are usually equally responsible for the employee's performance depending on which function they perform. For example, an employee might work in a specialized area in a business division dedicated to a product, service, geographical region, or customer. This structure is useful when a product or service is complex or is rapidly expanding. Businesses might choose this structure when the silos that exist within divisions no longer make the organization efficient. Furthermore, it is an optimal structure if rapid change is needed for a business to achieve a competitive advantage, whether that change requires more resources or additional expertise. In this manner, the business can focus more on the work that needs to be completed and a little less on the people in their silos. As a result, cost is typically minimized through the sharing of people and/or resources.

There are also disadvantages to this structure. For instance, reporting to more than one manager can be challenging, as responsibilities may be unclear or complicated. The matrix structure requires constant awareness, communication, and coordination between two or more managers to figure out an employee's work assignments and priorities. This could sometimes lead to conflicting messaging and demands, causing the employee's stress level to rise, resulting in a loss of efficiency as the work assignments are agreed upon. Matrix structures are common in project-driven organizations, or circumstances in which employees from different specialties form a team until the completion of the project, after which they return to their standard functions. From an HR perspective, ensuring fairness and equity can sometimes be tricky in a matrix structure because there are many reporting levels for employees.

A **divisional structure** basically separates an organization into parts. This could mean organizing a business by product or service and output. Divisions could also be further divided by geographical region. Each division is then responsible for everything related to that product, service, or region, depending upon how the business is structured. For example, a large beverage company might have three divisions: soda, water, and flavored seltzer. Each division would have its own departments, such as finance, marketing, and research and development. In other words, there could be identical departments in each division. Continuing with this example, soda would have separate departments for finance, marketing, and research and development. Water would also have separate departments for finance, marketing, and research and development, as would the flavored seltzer division.

This structure allows for intense focus and attention on each of the specialized services or products a company has and easy coordination within each specialized division, especially when compared with a hierarchical structure. Decision making is also faster in each functional area. The main disadvantage of divisional structure is that there is a duplication of effort, and some efficiencies could be lost between duplicated departments. From a financial perspective, different divisions might be competing against each other for the same customers, and procurement of supplies might cost more than if the divisions purchased together. Additionally, a divisional structure reduces the ability for employees in a certain department to benefit from the knowledge and continuing education from another identical department in a different division.

Summarize what is meant by an open boundary structure.

Summarize HR documents, their importance, and how to prepare them.

Summarize a SWOT analysis.

Explain how to visually represent a SWOT analysis.

Explain the link between HR and organizational strategy.

Explain strategic planning in HR, its importance, and how to develop a plan.

HR documentation is a key aspect of a well-functioning department and organization. Accurately preparing and maintaining HR documents can provide evidence and give the rationale behind different organizational decisions. This documentation can be used to help make a case in the event of a legal action or EEOC case.

HR documents encompass a myriad of work activities. When preparing HR-related documents, there are several things to keep in mind, the first of which is what type of document is being prepared. There should be records in areas such as recruiting, hiring, policies, medical files, benefit documents, personnel records, payroll data, disciplinary or performance records, leave records, and training materials. It will be important to understand what the compliance requirements are for the documentation. The individual preparing the document should know how long the documents must be retained, where they should be stored, who will be viewing the documents, and who will have access to them after completion. There are regulations surrounding the storage and retention of many HR documents. For example, an employer must keep an application on file for one year according to Title VII. I-9 forms and verification documents have different retention requirements as well. They should be maintained for three years after an employee is hired or for one year after an employee separates. The person responsible for maintaining documents should determine which of the two has the later date and use that as the guideline. Regarding storage, medical files should be housed separately from personnel files, so knowing which category certain prepared documents fall under is key.

An organization with an **open boundary structure** is established without traditional boundaries or divisions. In other words, there are none of the boxes or solid lines found in a typical organization chart. Instead, all units or functions are fluid and flexible. Traditional departments are more team-like, and the business—including suppliers—works closely together as one. This means that everyone can participate in decision making, as organizational hierarchy is almost nonexistent. The most important characteristic of an open boundary structure is the organization's ability to quickly adapt and be flexible in order to be as innovative as possible. Additionally, organizations with this structure are usually tech savvy, utilizing the latest and greatest technology, and have flexible working schedules that rely heavily on all forms of electronic communication.

The primary advantage of this structure is that it fully leverages everyone's talent, eliminates bureaucratic bottlenecks, and can adapt and change to market forces quickly. However, this type of structure needs strong leadership and vision because efficiencies based on specialty knowledge may not always be achieved and could be time-consuming to maintain.

SWOT analyses are usually represented visually in a table or matrix with four separate areas.

- Strengths:
    - What does the organization do well?
    - What resources does the organization have?
    - What is the competitive advantage?
- Weaknesses:
    - Where can the organization improve?
    - What limitations to resources exist?
    - What does the organization lack?
- Opportunities:
    - Is there a current need the organization could meet?
    - Are there requested products that could be provided?
    - Is there talent that could be hired?
- Threats
    - Are there regulation changes that could impact the organization?
    - Are competitors offering new products?
    - Is there dependence on a single supplier?

A SWOT analysis is used to identify and define the strengths, weaknesses, opportunities, and threats related to an organization, department, or project. This technique can be applied to a variety of fields. It is frequently used at an organizational level to ascertain how closely a business is aligned with its strategic objectives and benchmarks and to evaluate how it is placed competitively in the market. Strengths and weaknesses are internally focused, and opportunities and threats are external factors.

Strengths are internal factors about the organization that are positive, and that the organization can control. Strengths could include products, qualities, or practices that set the organization apart from competitors. Resources, such as a trained and knowledgeable staff, are considered strengths, as are things the organization does well. Tangible assets like proprietary processes or technology and intellectual property fall under the strengths category as well.

Weaknesses are internal factors about the organization that are considered adverse attributes or that deduct from the strengths. Weaknesses include areas where the company does not perform well. Limited or lacking resources are also weaknesses. Additional weaknesses can include low customer satisfaction rates or high levels of turnover.

Opportunities are external factors that could potentially contribute to success or higher performance. Opportunities can include areas such as potential growth rate in the industry, the ability to provide a new or requested product or service, advances in technology, the ability to hire talent, or the capacity to operate in a location where less competition exists.

Threats are external factors that cannot be controlled and could negatively affect success or lower performance. Threats can include costs of materials and supplies, changes to laws and regulations that impact the business, supply chain issues, and emerging competitors.

Strategic planning in HR refers to how HR professionals plan for both risks and opportunities by leveraging resources to meet HR initiatives and organizational objectives. The more closely aligned the HR department is with the business strategy, the closer the organization can get to anticipating and responding to needs, trends, and targets. This allows the organization to better maintain an advantage in its market. Planning, training, metrics, forecasting, and developing the workforce will aid the company in successfully achieving the business objectives and strategy. Strategic planning in HR can help promote productivity, keep employees aligned with strategic goals, address critical issues in a timely manner to avoid dilemmas, and help guide development and training. When developing an effective strategic plan, HR should be able to assess staffing levels and skills needed to not only meet and keep up with demands, but also keep up with changes in the technology and various processes. Performance management is another key area that needs to be adequately designed, to motivate and engage employees and focus them on the objectives and goals of the department and organization. Compensation is another important element, as competitive total compensation will help retain employees and could aid in attracting new talent.

Prior to developing a strategic plan, the HR department should assess the current situation, identify the desired future state, form and begin to implement frameworks to meet the strategic objectives, and determine how progress toward the objective is measured and evaluated. The SWOT analysis can be a key aid when developing the strategic plan, as the analysis can help provide understanding of the organization's current state. Additionally, a PESTLE analysis (political, economic, social, technological, legal, environmental) can be used to help provide a more detailed look at how external factors may impact the organization in the current state and over the long term. Solid strategic planning helps the organization achieve its mission, objectives, and goals while also maximizing productivity and profit.

Organizational strategy is a dynamic plan detailing the necessary actions that will enable the organization to achieve its short- and long-term goals. HR plays a critical role in an organization's strategic plan. Understanding an organization's strategy and how the business operates allows HR to better serve the organization's needs and human asset-related issues. Human capital impacts many aspects of a business, including recruitment, performance management, compensation and training, and development. HR must ensure that the correct people are aligned and performing in accordance with the organizational strategy adopted by the organization. There is a strong connection between HR, strategic planning, and implementation because HR must leverage human capital to optimize the success of an organization.

Explain why an organization would conduct an employee attitude survey.

Discuss some disadvantages an organization should consider before conducting an employee attitude survey.

Describe data collection for an employee engagement survey.

Summarize the key elements of a pulse survey.

Describe the structure and best practices of employee focus groups.

Explain the management by walking around strategy and explain why it is important for an organization to use it.

There are also some disadvantages an organization should consider before implementing an employee attitude survey:

- Surveys set the expectation that an employer will act upon its employees' responses. If the employer just wants to know employee thoughts and does not plan to implement changes or communicate rationales, then employee morale could drop.
- It could be time-consuming to design, implement, and evaluate the survey, and execute changes based on the results.
- Completing a survey could be thought of as an annoyance, and employees may choose not to participate, resulting in a low response rate that may not be worth the effort.
- Employees may not give undivided attention to the survey, or perhaps concentrate only on areas they view negatively, which could be misleading for employers.

An employer would conduct an employee attitude survey to better understand what employees think about the company and its work environment. Employee attitude surveys can measure either employee satisfaction or opinions on specific issues. Some of the information that might be collected and evaluated includes workplace culture, communication effectiveness, management effectiveness, safety at work, and specialized initiatives in the organization. There are many advantages for an organization to conduct an employee attitude survey:

- Employees like to feel valued, so asking them their perspective on a number of key topics helps them feel their voices count while also helping employers adjust course if necessary. Also, it demonstrates the organization cares about its employees.
- Employee attitude surveys are anonymous, which encourages honesty. Employers gain the honest opinions of employees because of this format. It provides a better understanding of the organization's strengths and weaknesses as viewed by employees.
- New ideas resulting from the survey could lead to better development and training programs.
- These surveys boost employee engagement and two-way communications.

A **pulse survey** is different from an employee attitude or engagement survey in that it is shorter (usually just a few questions), can measure anything, and can be administered more frequently. Hence, it lets an organization assess any specific topic more often. These short, usually easier-to-administer surveys also let an organization evaluate and act upon information quickly. Therefore, there is sentiment among employees that the organization is listening to them more and genuinely trying to implement changes that benefit the employees and the organization. As a result, employees feel valued, and the organization can continuously grow and improve.

Some of the topics a pulse survey might measure include effectiveness of business metrics, effectiveness of specific employer initiatives, and training effectiveness. Additionally, the questions can change from department to department and can be modified over time to measure progress in a specific area. For example, how likely is an employee to recommend the company as a place to work for friends and colleagues?

A pulse survey can be an effective tool to supplement an annual employee engagement survey and/or stand alone to measure specific aspects of progress. Pulse survey results are sometimes viewed as a monitoring tool.

An **employee engagement survey** is an empirical method for capturing what is in the hearts and minds of employees. It is usually conducted once a year. The survey is designed to measure aspects of employee engagement and is used as a tool to analyze the employee experience and drive change.

An employee engagement survey can be administered on paper or electronically, depending on the environment and employee access to technology. Employee engagement surveys typically range from 20 to 40 questions. There is no exact number of desired questions because that depends on the organization and what information is desired. A balance needs to be achieved between too few questions, which may not yield enough data, and too many questions, which might create an overabundance of data too complicated to summarize in reports. Usually, questions are written to measure engagement, determine what drives engagement, and provide the opportunity for open-ended questions and comments. Except for comments, responses can be indicated on a Likert scale of five ranking points that measures the degree to which an employee agrees or disagrees with a statement.

The **management by walking around** (MBWA) strategy is simply a method in which an organization encourages employee communication and involvement by making managers and supervisors readily available. An organization encourages managers and supervisors to traverse the workspace so they can check on the progress of each employee, discuss questions or concerns, and ultimately handle any problems that the employee or the manager identifies.

This strategy may appear to be extremely straightforward and relatively obvious because most organizations attempt to make sure that managers and supervisors are monitoring the progress of their employees. However, it is an important qualitative methodology for informally collecting information about what employees might be thinking. This is extremely useful during times of rapid changes, when observing and listening captures the essence or tone of issues that other methods of data collection might miss. This form of data collection usually requires active listening training for the manager and the ability to direct or redirect conversations in a nonconfrontational format to reveal the root of a problem or trends.

Focus groups can be used to glean employee views and concerns. They may be used to assess a new benefit plan or organizational change. Most focus groups contain 5 to 12 voluntary participants, with 3 to 10 groups in total. Participants should be informed about the subject of the focus group, about who will benefit, and that the information will be kept confidential. Participants may be selected at random or through the use of certain applicable filters. Focus group organizers should ensure that power differentials within the group are avoided. It is also important to involve participants from various levels of staff so they can fully represent the affected population. A neutral facilitator should be chosen to lead the discussion and ask open-ended, guided questions. Following the meeting, collected data should be analyzed and reported.

Explain how an organization can utilize a suggestion box for employee feedback.

Summarize the purpose of interviews.

Describe the types of interviews.

Describe a stay interview and its purpose.

Explain why and how an organization should conduct an exit interview.

Explain work-life balance.

The basic purpose of an interview is to obtain a certain amount of information from the interviewee concerning defined questions and issues. This give-and-take process is not merely words. Information can be gathered from gestures, body language, facial expressions, posture, and other nonverbal communication. Communication with words can be further dissected when tone, speech speed, and inflection are taken into consideration. An interview is a purposeful exchange between the interviewer and the interviewee that can be one-on-one, in groups, or any combination thereof. Generally, interviews tend to be more personal than surveys and allow the interviewer to probe further with follow-up questions and additional clarification if needed.

A suggestion box is a place, either physical or virtual, where employees can give their anonymous opinions about anything in the work environment or working conditions, or ways to improve efficiency or profitability. A suggestion box is a tool to help employees feel more engaged and involved, and to help the organization become a better place to work. A suggestion box improves communication, increases innovative thinking to help solve organizational problems, and could improve employee morale.

If the organization is using a physical box, then the box should be placed in a location where all employees have access. A physical box should also be locked shut, with access limited only to those with keys. If a virtual box is used, then IT needs to ensure suggestions are truly anonymous. Before implementing a suggestion box, an employer should be prepared to take it seriously by being welcoming of suggestions and eager to read and act on them. A program, including guidelines, should be developed to administer and promote the suggestion box. Additionally, incentives could be offered for participating. Employers should read suggestions on a regular basis and be sure to thank employees for their input.

A **stay interview** is a discussion between a manager and an employee in which the employer ascertains why a valued employee continues to work for the organization and if there is anything the employer can do to improve. The goal is to retain top talent and better understand what the organization is doing poorly, as well as learn what the organization is doing well. While employee satisfaction and engagement can be measured in an attitude survey, a stay interview allows for an immediate two-way conversation, enabling the employer to ask follow-up questions. Generally, stay interviews are conducted by employers once or twice during the onboarding process, typically over a six-month period; and then annually, usually six months apart from an employee's annual performance appraisal. The following are some questions an employer might ask during the approximately 30-minute stay interview:

- What do you enjoy about working here?
- What are a few things you look forward to every day?
- What can we do to make your job more satisfying?
- Do you feel valued and utilized in your current position?

The type of interview used depends on the situation and the preference of the interviewer. These are the most commonly used types of interviews:

- **Structured** interview—Every interviewee is asked the same questions. Similar information from interviewees can then be fairly compared to others.
- **Patterned** interview—Interviewees are asked different questions, but all questioning the same body of knowledge, skill, or ability.
- **Stress** interview—The interviewer is aggressive in approach to see how an interviewee might respond. Stress interviews are frequently used in law enforcement.
- **Directive** interview—A structured interview in which the interviewer asks very specific questions in a calm, controlled manner.
- **Nondirective** interview—The interviewer asks more open-ended questions in a particular direction, but the interviewees can drive the direction of questions. These are frequently used in counseling.
- **Behavioral** interview—The interviewer asks specific questions about past behavior, performance, and examples as a way to gauge the interviewee's skill set and knowledge. Typically, past performance can be a good indicator of future performance.
- **Situational** interview—The interviewer asks questions that require the interviewee to consider situations he or she may have experienced in a certain role and how it was handled, thereby gauging an interviewee's knowledge and skills.

Work-life balance is generally defined as the competing prioritization between one's personal and professional activities. Advances in technology have meant that a physical office location no longer always needs to be the primary place to accomplish work-related tasks; this, in turn, has made the juggling act of work-life balance an increasingly hot topic. A poor work-life balance can lead to employee stress and burnout, diminished productivity, and lost revenue. Therefore, it is in the organization's best interest to share some of the responsibility for improving the balance between work and an employee's personal life.

Some business leaders maintain that, due to technological advances that everyone should strive for, a "work-life integration" should be the true end goal because complete separation might not be realistic. Achieving a balance then becomes a shared responsibility with the employee and the employer.

Exit interviews are opportunities for organizations to gather honest feedback about why an employee is choosing to leave the organization. Exit interviews are almost always encouraged because they yield information that may help the organization improve and retain employees in the future. In most organizations, a member of the HR team, acting as an impartial and neutral party (and not as the employee's direct supervisor), conducts the exit interview to put the employee at ease. The following are ways to make an exit interview as productive as possible:

- Try to make the employee feel comfortable. Remind them that their input is extremely valuable and thank them for their time and expertise.
- Ask open-ended questions and repeat responses to ensure understanding. Yes-or-no questions should be avoided, and notes should be taken about what the employee said and did not say.
- The most important question to ask is why the employee started to look for another job.

Typically, HR analyzes and summarizes the information obtained from an exit interview and shares the information with the organization's leadership team to examine areas for improvement.

Summarize some of the ways an employer can help employees achieve a good work-life balance.

Summarize the characteristics of a virtual or remote work environment.

Explain the advantages and disadvantages of a virtual or remote work environment.

Describe some legal considerations an employer should consider when devising and managing work-life balance programs.

Explain sabbatical leave and its advantages and disadvantages for an employer.

Summarize the characteristics of an organization's recognition programs.

A virtual work environment is possible thanks to technological advancements that have reduced employers' need for a physical, brick-and-mortar presence or office space. Virtual work environments allow employees to work in remote locations, including homes, coffee shops, or anywhere that connectivity can be achieved. Work units or teams can collaborate via virtual networks and accomplish work via many formats, such as video conferencing, phone, and virtual servers to share and store information. Employers are starting to include virtual or remote policies in their employee handbooks that define expectations when working remotely, with new protocols regarding start time, end time, meal breaks, check-in procedures, etc. Some employers have more informal plans, such as a quick video conference in the morning or at the end of the day, casual conversation to see how everyone on a team is doing, or manager office hours. Due to advances in technology and the cost savings achieved from remote work, the trend is that the virtual workplace is growing.

Generally, the US Equal Employment Opportunity Commission (EEOC) supports work-life balance programs. However, if the program is not implemented fairly, it could violate Title VII of the Civil Rights Act, requiring equal treatment and preventing discrimination. Some work-life balance programs are left to the discretion of a manager or HR representative. If an employee requests a flexible working arrangement and the manager is not consistent and fair in administering these requests, the disappointed employee may claim unlawful discrimination. Furthermore, there is the risk of an inconsistent or unfair decision resulting in disparate treatment or disparate impact against a protected class or classes. In addition, an employee could ask for a flexible work arrangement due to a family or medical condition that would otherwise be covered under the Family and Medical Leave Act (FMLA). If the request meets the specific requirements of FMLA, then it should be processed accordingly to avoid legal consequences. Another legal consideration is whether the employee is making the request due to a disability. In this case, the employer may be in violation of the Americans with Disabilities Act (ADA), and the request should have been processed and determined via a reasonable accommodation. Lastly, flexible work arrangements carry the potential for Fair Labor Standards Act (FLSA) wage and hour issues or violations, especially when calculating hours worked. These types of legal matters, along with ongoing changes in federal, state, and local laws, should always be considered when a business implements a work-life balance program.

Recognition programs are an important part of the employee experience that enhance employee engagement and help positively shape company culture. Recognition should be tailored to the organization and its employees—there is not a one-size-fits-all plan. However, the goal of most recognition programs is to help make employees feel valued or appreciated, and they frequently serve as an incentive to strive toward. Recognition programs can reward any number of desirable attributes or events, such as going above and beyond, team effort, wellness objectives, innovation, quality improvements, and career celebrations. Recognition rewards can vary, but may include the following:

- A heartfelt, verbal (or written) thank-you
- A meal celebration
- A point-based system for employees to choose a reward
- Treats or candy
- Gift cards
- Unique experiences such as concerts, sporting events, or shows

A recognition program provides an employer with the ability to create a workplace of choice where employees thrive. Recruitment and employee retention is positively influenced by an effective recognition program. Successful recognition has the following characteristics: recognition is genuine, all employees have an opportunity to give and receive recognition, the reward is given in a timely manner, it is specific, it is connected to the company's purpose, and it is presented in a public forum. There are also software programs and vendors that can help an organization design and administer recognition programs.

An employer can help its employees in a number of different ways, depending on the needs of the business. A **flexible work arrangement** could mean working remotely, scheduling outside typical business hours, part-time arrangements, telecommuting on certain days, job sharing, and shift swapping. Businesses that adopt such measures may experience reduced turnover, increased productivity, and the ability to recruit from an expanded talent pool. In some situations, flexible work arrangements are not possible due to the nature of the business. If that is the case, businesses can also promote campaigns to encourage breaks, regularly review workload balance, and take time off; lead by example; provide resources for working parents; or offer other perks to ease the burden for their employees.

There is not a one-size-fits-all approach for employers to assist workers in finding their individual work-life balance; rather, the program should be customized for the business, as well as recognizing that every employee is different with diverse circumstances. Work-life balance programs can give businesses a competitive advantage, but if poorly designed and implemented, or managed incorrectly, the program could unintentionally harm morale and/or be legally detrimental to the company.

There are many advantages to a virtual or remote work environment:
- Cost effectiveness—Working virtually enables companies to have lower operating costs and be more environmentally friendly. Examples include smaller workspace and less commuting, which respectively cost less to maintain and expend less energy.
- Flexibility—Working remotely or at home is a perk for many employees because it eliminates commuting and promotes better work-life balance.
- Improved productivity—Employees who can better balance their work and personal life tend to be happier, and research indicates that happier employees tend to be more productive. Remote work also eliminates many of the distractions that occur in an in-person office environment.
- Bigger talent pool—Virtual work environments mean that recruiting is not restricted by location. This enables an employer to cast a wider net for top talent.

There are also some disadvantages to virtual or remote work environments:
- Preference—Some employees may not like working remotely or do not have a space or environment that is conducive to productively accomplishing work. Remote work can be isolating, and many have a hard time separating work and personal life when working from home.
- Difficulties collaborating—Sometimes there is no substitute for face-to face collaboration. It could take time to figure out ways to make virtual collaboration work well.
- Trust—Employers can monitor technology to see if an employee is active, but there needs to be a level of trust between the employer and employee for this work arrangement to work.

A **sabbatical leave** is generally a paid leave from an organization to work on a long-term project. This is typically a four-week to three-month leave to concentrate solely on the project without distraction. Sabbatical leave used to only apply to professors or researchers in academic environments. There has been a slow shift to allow this type of leave in other industries for professional development, authoring articles, etc. Sabbatical leave is usually reserved for more senior, longer-term employees who already have years of experience, but there are no specific legal regulations and few case-law precedents for sabbatical implementation. It is wise for organizations to have clearly defined criteria and guidelines when offering sabbatical leave to employees in order to ensure it is implemented in a fair and consistent manner.

There are many advantages for an organization to offer sabbaticals: they attract top talent; give employers a competitive edge; demonstrate that an employer cares for their employees, thereby promoting loyalty; and promote long-term retention of employees. There are also some disadvantages: cost; decreased productivity due to an employee's absence; administrative challenge to maintain benefits; potential conflict or resentment among employees covering the workload; and the possibility that the employee on sabbatical will not return to work.

Explain how companies use special events to build a positive work culture.

Discuss the key components and best practices of performance management systems.

Explain the process of setting performance goals.

Summarize what is meant by setting "SMART" performance goals.

Briefly explain why documenting employee performance is critical.

Explain benchmarking and its usage in HR.

Performance management is the HR function concerned with setting performance standards, evaluating employee effectiveness against those standards, identifying any problem areas, and implementing interventions to correct problems. Performance management is vital because an organization cannot thrive if individuals, teams, and departments aren't effective in their roles.

The performance management process can vary from one organization to another, but most firms follow three basic steps:

- Through activities like goal-setting, needs analysis, and the creation of a corporate value statement and code of conduct, company leaders and HR professionals establish organizational goals. They then identify the knowledge, skills, behaviors, and tasks required to achieve those goals and inform employees how to best work to meet those company objectives.
- The firm's management then needs to monitor employee performance, document any problems, and help employees correct those problems if possible.
- At predetermined intervals, typically once a year, managers will conduct in-depth performance appraisals for each employee. These appraisals measure performance during the preceding period. Often, the manager and employee will set goals for the employee to work toward in the new appraisal period.

SMART is an acronym that stands for "specific, measurable, achievable, relevant, and timebound." The idea is that every goal an employee sets should be SMART:

- **Specific**—The goal should clearly define what is to be achieved as specifically as possible. For example, a goal to "improve diversity in the company" is not specific at all, but a goal to "begin an electronic diversity awareness monthly communication about a different aspect of diversity" is very specific.
- **Measurable**—Performance goals should be quantifiable in some unit of measurement. For example, "reduce return processing" isn't measurable, but "reduce return processing time by 10 percent before December 31" has a clear and unmistakable deadline.
- **Achievable**—A goal should be a challenge for the employee and require a high level of effort, but should also be reasonable and realistic.
- **Relevant**—All performance goals should link to organizational goals.
- **Timebound**—There needs to be a due date or period of time in which the goal will be achieved. Time is usually reflected as a specific date or numeric period, like December 31 or the end of the third fiscal quarter.

Benchmarking is a process or system by which an organization measures its performance against other similar business groupings considered to have best practices, sometimes called "best in class." In order to grow, companies must compare given functions and practices to the best in class in order to improve efficiencies and productivity. In HR, benchmarking is frequently used to compare an organization in the areas of recruitment, employee retention, salary, performance, employee engagement, HR strategies, etc.

An organization can choose to conduct **internal benchmarking,** whereby they closely examine and compare the efficiencies realized in their own organization, or **external benchmarking,** which involves an organization comparing its functional information against other industries. The objective is to discover what areas of the business could benefit from improvement to hopefully maintain a competitive advantage and cultivate a culture of continuous improvement. Some specific benefits of benchmarking may include lowered labor cost, increase in sales and profits, operational efficiencies, increased productivity, and quality improvements. Benchmarking may be the impetus that drives change, so organizations must prepare accordingly with change management education in the organization.

Company-sponsored special events can vary, but all serve as a way to leverage and promote employee engagement and build a positive company culture. Some special events can be recurring, such as holiday dinners, summer picnics, Friday social nights, or Tuesday tacos in the office. These events may be social outings with or without employee family members. However, they serve to build camaraderie among employee team members and give them opportunities to socialize with one another outside of the work environment. This may help build a stronger, more productive work team, as well as improve employee satisfaction. Events can also incorporate an element of community service, including serving food at a local soup kitchen, volunteering at an animal shelter, or building homes for those in need. Some special events might also include wellness-related campaigns, company walking or running teams, weight loss or healthy eating initiatives, or yoga classes at lunch. Special events demonstrate that the employer cares about the employees' health and well-being.

A performance goal is a written declaration of an anticipated end result in a specified period of time. These goals are usually discussed between an employee and their manager. Performance goals are then chosen and agreed upon based on company objectives and/or the employee's personal aspirations. Goals are desired outcomes that specify defined measures such as time frame, quantity, quality, or a percentage. Employee performance goals should link into and support the overall strategic plan of the company or unit, and at the same time should assist in keeping the employee engaged and motivated. It is an opportunity for an employee to formulate a plan with their manager to focus on those job duties, responsibilities, and tasks that will best enable individual achievement of goals that carefully integrate with company goals. To be effective, performance goals should be evaluated and re-evaluated in a timely fashion, perhaps every quarter, six months, or annually. Performance goals are not written in stone and can be updated or revised as needed to maintain motivation over time.

Up-to-date performance documentation is important to maintain in an employee's personnel file, as it frequently demonstrates the reasoning behind why decisions, both positive and negative, were made. This documentation is especially useful in an employee's performance appraisal because it demonstrates performance with examples. Some managers find it useful to keep a performance diary, documenting a record of key activities or tasks executed by the employee.

Employee performance documentation is essential in the event of a lawsuit. Furthermore, the documentation must be accurate, objective, and specific. The following are some guidelines to maintain when documenting employee performance:

- Document right away to avoid anything being forgotten.
- Keep notes on all employees.
- Separate fact from opinion.
- Make sure notes are objective.
- Remove emotion from documentation.
- Be respectful when writing.

Performance documentation is not only useful to avoid possible legal issues, but it can also be leveraged to improve an employee's performance and to create a professional development plan or possibly reward outstanding performance.

Explain a balanced scorecard.

Briefly discuss techniques for giving performance feedback.

Discuss the role of performance management software.

Describe some of the main types of performance appraisal methods.

Name and describe the three main forms of ranking.

Identify and describe some rating appraisal methods.

How performance feedback is delivered plays a vital role in how it is received and subsequent outcomes. First, whenever possible, feedback should be given in private and always in a respectful manner. It is important to remember that feedback is not negative. Rather, performance feedback is an opportunity for a supervisor to discuss information that should help make the employee more productive and provide clear direction and priorities moving forward. This should be a two-way discussion and not a supervisor speaking at length to a silent employee. It is important for a manager not to come across as overbearing or cruel, but rather approach feedback in a manner that is sincerely helpful. The manager giving feedback should actively listen to the employee and recap or clarify what the employee is saying if needed, as well as empathize with the employee's point of view.

A manager should be cognizant that the words used to describe an undesired behavior are factual, not judgmental. For example, "Ann, could you just stop making so many errors on the same XYZ activity? Try harder!" is judgmental. However, "Ann, it seems there are some issues doing XYZ. What are your thoughts?" is better. A manager should be specific when providing feedback, both positive and negative. For example, "Derrick, you are doing a good job!" isn't specific; instead, a manager should say something like, "Derrick, your closing numbers are great, 35 percent above the department average, and with 98 percent customer satisfaction ratings. That's awesome!"

There are many different performance appraisal methods. Some involve feedback from the immediate supervisor, and some involve the feedback of peers, clients, or subordinates. Many organizations begin the process with self-appraisals. **Self-appraisals** are most beneficial when used for personal development and identifying training needs, but less beneficial when they are used as a basis for the formal evaluation process. Good supervisors are able to evaluate performance and give meaningful feedback. Hence, it should not be surprising that **supervisor appraisals** are typically required as at least one major component of the overall performance appraisal process. One type of appraisal that considers feedback from multiple sources is a **360-degree appraisal**. These appraisals have rapidly grown in popularity and are expected to share a broader perspective of performance because they include feedback from everyone the employee interacts with—managers, peers, clients, and subordinates.

There are a variety of rating appraisal methods, but the two most common are the checklist method and the rating scale method. The **checklist method** is a series of statements describing a certain level of performance. The performance evaluator can then check a box next to the statement that best describes the individual's performance in each performance area. The **rating scale method** rates an individual's performance on a point scale, usually a 1–3, 1–4, 1–5, or 1–10 scale, with higher numbers representing better performance.

The **balanced scorecard** is a strategic performance management tool that was developed by Robert Kaplan and David Norton in 1996. The tool is designed to identify, report, and improve an organization through four perspectives in time:

- **Financial**—How various stakeholders view the organization
- **Customer**—How customers view the organization
- **Business process**—What the organization excels at
- **Learning and growth**—How the organization continuously improves

This tool and subsequent reports can be used by leadership and management to better monitor the actions or activities within their span of control and keep track of the results.

The performance management process needs to be effective to be productive. If the process is too cumbersome, then there is the risk it becomes a "check-the-box" routine and not as productive as it could be. The end goal is to improve the performance of employees. Many companies utilize various forms and formats of performance management software, both web-based and mobile, to augment the process for efficiency. Software can vary, but most programs enable the manager to easily keep a record of all performance-related discussions, track progress against goals, and illustrate how progress against goals is linked to the company's strategic objectives. Most also provide a way of capturing skills for each employee, which in turn can assist with succession planning in case an employee leaves the organization. Many even have the capability to facilitate 360-degree feedback between managers, employees, and peers. Additionally, most software packages can produce helpful dashboards, illustrating progress and standard and customized reports to assist management when evaluating performance. Performance management software can be a stand-alone product or part of a more integrated and robust HR system.

Ranking procedures put employees in order from highest to lowest based upon evaluation characteristics such as performance. There are three main forms of ranking:

- **Straight ranking** involves listing all employees in order, with number one being the best, number two being second best, number three being third, and so on.
- **Alternate ranking** entails choosing the best and the worst from a list of all employees, removing these names from the list, and repeating until there are no names left.
- **Paired comparison** consists of evaluating only two employees at a time, deciding which is better, and continuing until each employee has been paired against every other employee.

Ranking procedures assist with distributing budgeted pay increases that are more clearly tied to performance, and they eliminate some of the biases found in traditional review criteria. The forced-distribution method, also known as **forced ranking**, uses a bell curve in which the majority of employees will receive an average score and a small group will receive extremely high or extremely low performance scores.

Name and describe the three main behaviorally based appraisal methods.

Identify and describe some narrative appraisal methods.

Describe some common errors that can occur in the performance appraisal process.

Describe performance appraisals and how to avoid bias in them.

Summarize legal considerations in the performance appraisal process.

Describe the role of an ethical agent.

The three most common narrative appraisal techniques are the critical incident method, the essay method, and the field review method.

The **critical incident method** documents each performance problem related to an employee occurring during a set period so that the evaluator can discuss problems with the employee at the end.

The **essay method** requires performance evaluators to write a short essay about each employee describing their performance during the period in question.

The **field review method** is a method in which an individual other than the employee's direct supervisor or manager performs the appraisal and writes down a series of assessments and observations about that employee's performance.

Greater focus on accountability and results has led to new approaches for appraising performance. The three main **behaviorally based appraisal methods** are management by objectives, behaviorally anchored rating scales, and behavioral observation scales.

Management by objectives is proactive rather than reactive. It focuses on predicting and shaping the future of the company, accomplishing results rather than simply following directions, improving competence and effectiveness, and increasing the participation and engagement of employees.

Behaviorally anchored rating scales (BARS) assign numerical values to performance based on a given range, such as a five-star system or a scale from 1 to 10. The BARS method analyzes the job description for a particular position and identifies the tasks that must be performed for the organization to function effectively. Once the tasks are identified, a determination is made about the specific way the individual should behave to perform each task. For example, if communication is identified as a necessary skill for a management position, then an individual in that position must be able to keep others informed. A series of ranked statements are then designed to describe how effectively the individual performed. Performance appraisers can choose the statement that best describes the employee's behavior. The key benefits of BARS are that they create agreement by being less subjective and more based upon observations.

Behavioral observation scales are similar to BARS, but with greater focus on frequency of behavior than on quality of performance, such as a sliding scale of "always," "sometimes," and "never."

Performance appraisals are a key part of employee feedback and development. However, it is very difficult to be 100% objective when completing such an evaluation, and inevitably, some bias may seep in. Both conscious and unconscious bias during the review process can have a negative impact on the employee and on the organization. Reviews that are inflated or deflated can lead to skewed metrics, with unreliable readings on true performance levels in the organization.

In order to combat bias in performance appraisals, there are several things to keep in mind. Those responsible for rating others should be reminded to think critically about their own biases and assumptions so they can avoid having them affect their assessments. Leaders should provide their team members with regular feedback, which will help prevent recency bias. Regular feedback also provides contextual information to refer back to during formal appraisals and ensures nothing during the appraisals comes as a shock.

Previous appraisals should be reviewed to check for patterns and trends that might indicate bias. Leaders need to be mindful and review the language used in the appraisal, as certain adjectives and phrases can demonstrate various types of bias. Metrics should be gathered to support feedback and should be incorporated in the report. Having hard data can eliminate some of the emotions involved in evaluations and can help eliminate bias. Feedback should be gathered from various sources such as peers, direct reports, and departments the employee may work with closely. Employees should also be asked to complete self-assessments, which can provide insights into areas where the rater might not have much knowledge or oversight.

Errors can occur when assessing employee performance. It is important to be aware of and hopefully avoid the following common errors:

- **Recency and primacy error**—A **recency** error is when the appraiser evaluates an employee on their more recent activities and not earlier performance. A **primacy** error is when an appraiser values an employee's earlier performance with greater emphasis than their more recent performance.
- **Halo and horn effect**—A **halo** effect is when an employee is exemplary in one area and rated outstanding because of the one area of expertise, ignoring other categories. A **horn** effect is just the opposite, where one area of weakness overshadows all other areas.
- **Strictness and leniency**—Some appraisers may believe the agreed-upon standards for performance are too low and therefore do not rate performance in a fair manner. In other words, they are reluctant to give the highest rating because, from their perspective, no one is ever that good. **Strictness** gives no room for failure. Conversely, **leniency** is when an appraiser gives an undeserving employee an inflated appraisal.
- **Bias**—This occurs when an appraiser's prejudices and values cloud their judgment, causing them to evaluate someone's performance through their own belief system and not necessarily the organization's.

Ethics are the moral principles, values, and accepted standards of behavior that determine whether an action is right or wrong. The Society for Human Resource Management (SHRM) Competency Model defines ethical practice as "the knowledge, skills, abilities, and other characteristics needed to maintain high levels of personal and professional integrity and to act as an ethical agent who promotes core values, integrity, and accountability throughout the organization."

Ethics and compliance officers ensure that business is conducted in accordance with rules, legal regulations, and industry standards of practice. Additionally, an ethical agent makes moral judgments based on fundamental ethical principles that are rooted in their personal character, not based on a situation's potential gains. Ethical dilemmas occur when a corporation or individual is faced with a conflict of interest, or actions that are blatantly wrong, deceptive, or may have uncertain consequences. Many ethical conflicts value profit over moral principles. Over the past few decades, ethics and business conduct have received increasing attention that has led to more stringent compliance regulations, like the Sarbanes-Oxley Act.

The EEOC clearly explains that performance appraisals, in accordance with Uniform Guidelines, must be job-related. Additionally, in a performance appraisal, careful attention is necessary to avoid any form of discrimination covered under Title VII of the Civil Rights Act of 1964 and related anti-discrimination laws. Evaluation criteria should be formally assessed in a structured format that limits subjective responses and increases the validity of data about performance. The goal is for performance to be rated against objective, predefined standards. Information and documentation must be based on genuine interaction with the employee being appraised. Furthermore, the actual appraisal meeting should have some mechanism or protocol in place to prevent one manager from dominating the discussion and unfairly influencing employee rating. Overall, the performance appraisal process should be equitable and fair for all employees.

Explain the importance of a code of conduct.

Visit *mometrix.com/academy* for a related video.
Enter video code: 391843

Define absenteeism and its impact on a business.

Explain aggressive behavior in the workplace.

Explain what an organization can do to maintain a safe work environment.

Summarize ways to deal with employee conflict.

Define insubordination and how to address it if it occurs.

Absenteeism is when employees do not arrive at work when scheduled. **Tardiness**, a form of absenteeism, occurs when an employee arrives late for work. Absenteeism and tardiness both negatively impact an organization's productivity, financial performance, and administrative cost to operate. Taking pre-approved time off for personal reasons or vacation is a benefit, and time for an employee to "recharge" away from work is beneficial. Additionally, the organization's management team knows in advance and can plan accordingly. Time off for illness usually cannot be predicted and is generally encouraged in order to not make an entire office sick. Also, there are many legal protections afforded an employee for illness-related absences.

Absenteeism is usually regarded as habitual time off for either legitimate or illegitimate reasons. Employers can develop policies for absenteeism that might involve improving communications about their excusable and inexcusable absences, one-on-one discussions with the employee, and recognition programs to reward good attendance. However, an employer should be careful when disciplining an employee for excessive absenteeism to ensure the discipline is not in violation with federal, state, or local laws and regulations, such as USERRA for military leave, occurrences covered under the Family and Medical Leave Act (FMLA), and other protected activities depending on state laws (voting, children's activities, medical).

A **code of conduct** is a set of behavioral rules rooted in moral standards, laws, and best practices that a company develops, adopts, and communicates to employees. It outlines expected behavior and defines what behavior will not be tolerated. The document should also state what disciplinary actions employees could face if they violate the code.

Employee involvement in the development of a code of conduct will lead to greater employee buy-in and adherence. The code should be written in clear language that can be applied to specific situations as they arise. Upon finalization, the code should be shared with all employees. Employees should then be required to sign a document acknowledging receipt and understanding of the new code.

The following are some options for organizations addressing aggressive behavior:

- Educate employees about safety and zero tolerance for violence, including resources such as an HR contact, a company security group, and key phone numbers or websites for help. Tell employees not to do anything or go anywhere they feel unsafe.
- Maintain vigilant security at the work site—surveillance cameras, identification tags, electronic entry, etc.
- Conduct training programs or offer resources to de-stress.

There is not a specific remedy if aggressive behavior is observed because it is dependent on a number of factors. Nevertheless, when encountering aggressive behavior, try to stay calm and de-escalate if possible, and never hesitate to call the police for assistance.

Aggressive behavior in the workplace is typically a response to stress that should be recognized and handled immediately before it causes more harm. Aggression and violence could be displayed in any number of ways, such as physical assault, intimidation, threats, stalking, property damage, or verbal or written abuse. It can also occur between employees, between an employee and customer, between an employee and a family member, or from an outsider who has ideological differences with the business, among other possibilities.

The US Department of Labor maintains that some people work in and around circumstances that present a greater danger of violence than others: people who handle cash, work in high-crime areas, or deliver services or goods. There are many triggers for aggression to occur, including money issues, job loss, demotion, personal loss, and holidays. Sometimes, there is nothing an employer can do to prevent aggression or violence, like a terrorist incident. Other times, there are warning signs that an employee might become aggressive at work, such as unexplained drastic changes in behavior, absenteeism, performance decline, chatter about unfair treatment, overly emotional reactions to situations, or expressions of paranoia. The goal is to recognize the signs and address them, usually with a zero-tolerance policy for aggressive or violent behavior.

Insubordination is when an employee overtly refuses to do or comply with a reasonable work request from their manager. The manager's request must meet two basic criteria: (1) the employee must thoroughly understand the request, and (2) the request cannot be dangerous or unethical. Claims of insubordination must be thoroughly investigated by HR from a position of neutrality, and a conclusion must be drawn as to why the employee is refusing to complete the assignment. The incident should be documented.

If this is a one-time occurrence that is unlikely to happen again, then a discussion of ways to behave going forward is appropriate. However, if insubordination becomes a pattern, then disciplinary action should be followed—possibly a verbal warning, a written warning, a suspension, or a combination of other similar alternatives. Termination is even possible if no other remediation helps to rectify the situation. Insubordination should always be thoroughly investigated, documented, and addressed immediately and appropriately, before it leads to a decline in productivity, possible employee turnover, or a hostile work environment.

Employee conflict, or disagreement among employees, will occur. Not all conflict is unproductive. Many times, employee disagreement or conflict that occurs in a constructive, respectful manner leads to innovation, increased creativity, and ultimately improvements. However, there are times when the opposite occurs and employee conflict is a negative experience for all involved. The following are some strategies for an organization to address negative employee conflict:

- Ask questions and gain a complete understanding of the problem. First, evaluate whether the conflict involves any EEOC violations, such as discrimination or harassment. Assuming no EEOC violations, gain an understanding of the root cause of the problem, not the fallout. Depending on the situation, encourage employees to work it out on their own, if possible. This is a judgment call.
- If intervention becomes necessary to prevent escalation, do so immediately. Listen to both sides, ask questions, and restate issues for clarification. Make sure both parties understand that they must let each other speak uninterrupted and address each other with respect. Encourage both parties to devise a way to manage going forward, and assist in devising a written plan that both agree to follow. Reference the employee handbook for behavioral expectations.
- Offer training or personality assessments to help conflicted employees improve their communication style, and encourage managers to lead by example.

Explain illegal harassment other than sexual harassment.

Discuss why it is important to conduct harassment training.

Summarize what is meant by bullying in the workplace and what to do about it.

Explain the guiding principles when approaching employee discipline.

Explain the importance of tracking employee grievances.

Summarize what is meant by progressive discipline.

Companies should conduct regular harassment training because employers must exercise reasonable care to avoid and prevent harassment. Several states have mandatory harassment training for certain types of employees. Otherwise, employers may be found liable for the harassing behaviors of vendors, clients, coworkers, and supervisors. **Harassment** is defined as any demeaning or degrading comments, jokes, name-calling, actions, graffiti, or other belittling conduct that may be found offensive. Any form of derogatory speech can be considered harassment, including neutral words that may be perceived in a vulgar or intimidating way. Furthermore, the Civil Rights Act of 1964 protects individuals from harassment on the basis of race, color, religion, gender, or national origin. Damages awarded under Title VII can total anywhere from $50,000 to $300,000, depending upon the size of the employer.

Illegal harassment usually involves unwelcome verbal exchanges, unwelcome physical contact, or unwelcome actions that are based on a person's race, religion, gender, sexual orientation, national origin, age, disability, genetic information, military membership, or veteran status. The action(s) taken must meet the threshold of a "severe and pervasive" work environment, characterized as hostile, abusive, or intimidating for "a reasonable person." If this type of harassment is present, it could be a violation of the following federal regulations: Title VII of the Civil Rights Act of 1964, the Americans with Disabilities Act (ADA), the Age Discrimination in Employment Act (ADEA), the Genetic Information Nondiscrimination Act (GINA), or the Uniformed Services Employment and Reemployment Rights Act (USERRA). Additionally, many states and local laws provide even more enhanced legal protections against harassment. Harassment interferes with an employee's ability to accomplish their work. All allegations of harassment should be reported, investigated immediately, and acted upon appropriately by the employer.

Discipline in the workplace is necessary, but should always be fair and within the constraints of federal, state, and local laws. To paraphrase an old proverb, "the punishment should fit the crime." All discipline should be applied consistently, or the organization is at risk for a legal violation. Additionally, it is a good practice to document a record of facts, including dates, leading to the disciplinary action, and steps taken to remedy the situation. An HR professional should be in a position to support any disciplinary actions. Asking questions to clarify when in doubt is an important step. An employee may not always agree with the action, but they must understand why corrective actions are needed. Being firm and consistent, and showing respect and empathy toward the employee, are necessary when discipline must be deployed.

Bullying is a form of aggressive behavior in the workplace that includes numerous forms of mistreatment that allow the bully to assert control and attack another person's self-confidence or self-esteem. Bullying can be overt, such as yelling, obscene language, and public humiliation. However, bullying can also be much more subtle, such as failing to invite a targeted employee to an essential meeting, withholding needed resources, sabotage, micromanagement, and inequitable treatment. In either case, while bullying is obviously detrimental to the victim, it may also damage the business by harming productivity or incurring legal costs. Many organizations have modified their harassment policies to specifically address bullying. Changing the policy needs to be combined with an awareness campaign so that employees understand what bullying is, what its consequences are, and how to report it. There should be a process for reporting claims of bullying—such as a contact in HR—so that the victim feels comfortable. All reported bullying incidents should be investigated immediately and, if necessary, met with action. Also, Title VII of the Civil Rights Act of 1964 and the EEOC could offer protections against harassment in the form of bullying, depending on the circumstances and investigative findings.

Progressive discipline is a method to inform an employee about behavior, conduct, or job performance that is unsatisfactory and to gradually implement actions designed to improve their behavior or performance. This gives the employee the opportunity to correct the undesired behavior or poor performance through a gradual progression of disciplinary responses. The goal of this process is to get the employee back on track toward becoming a more productive member of the organization.

There is not a specific formula for implementing progressive discipline. Usually, the seriousness of the infraction and number of incidents factor into the implementation of progressive discipline. Progressive discipline is typically a five-step process:

1. A **verbal warning**, or a one-on-one session with a manager reviewing the issues and the corrective action
2. A **written warning**, in which a manager documents the issue and lack of improvement
3. A **performance improvement plan (PIP)**, which is a documented plan that is time-bound and details what will happen if corrective action is not achieved
4. **Suspension**, for when a corrective action is not achieved and the employee is given time away from work to reflect on the situation
5. **Termination**, at which point the progressive discipline is labeled a failure and the employee is terminated

The overall rationale behind progressive discipline is to ensure employees are treated fairly and to help nurture a positive organizational culture.

A **grievance** is a complaint, by an employee to an employer, of some type of unfair treatment or violation. An employee grievance can be formal, like a written report, or informal, like a verbal discussion. Generally, a grievance can be from an employee against an employer or management official, from an employee against another employee, or any combination thereof. Some examples of grievances might include harassment, discrimination, safety concerns, workplace relationships, and organizational changes.

HR is often involved and tracks grievances, both for awareness and to determine if there are trends in grievances pointing to a bigger issue in an organization, such as a large number of grievances against one manager. Tracking grievances based on subject matter can assist in implementing quicker corrective actions. Measuring the time it takes to close a grievance could also impact employee satisfaction with the organization. If the problem is quickly addressed and resolved in a fair and expedient time frame, then the employee will feel more valued and satisfied. Tracking grievances also provides the organization a picture of whether employee complaints and grievances are rising or falling, which is another measure of organizational health.

Describe the difference between policies, procedures, and work rules.

Summarize issues to consider when delivering disciplinary action.

Explain a warning in a progressive discipline process.

Summarize what it means to have escalating corrective actions.

Describe termination in the progressive discipline process.

Explain wrongful termination.

Disciplinary actions, whether part of a union contract or not, should always be fair to all. Therefore, employees should have a process or ability to defend their actions against any accusation of wrongdoing. In other words, employees should be given the opportunity to present their side of the story in their words. An employer should be consistent in delivering discipline, meaning that treatment is similar to what others have received for equivalent offenses. A manager should always be able to produce strong, preferably documented, evidence of an employee's wrongdoing.

Disciplinary actions are rarely straightforward, and are usually complicated by other factors that must be taken into consideration. HR usually reviews disciplinary actions before they are implemented, trying to mitigate risk for the company. The following are some considerations HR should examine: any EEO violations; consistency in treatment; potential tort or other legal liabilities; compliance with union contracts (if applicable); and compliance with federal, state, and local laws and regulations.

The goal of an organization's policies, procedures, and work rules is to help an organization achieve its goals in an equitable and efficient manner. However, there is a difference between the three terms:

- **Policy**—An overarching or broad statement describing the company's basic philosophy and standards for all related management and employee activities. For example, a company might have a policy stating that "The company will reimburse for educational tuition if the course is related to work the employee performs. All coursework must be pre-approved by the management team." This is a broad statement that explains the policy for tuition reimbursement, but doesn't give specifics—it only states that there is an educational reimbursement policy.
- **Procedure**—This specifies very specific steps or methods to process or handle employee activities. For example, if an employee wants reimbursement for taking a course, they might have to follow these steps: (1) Meet with immediate supervisor to discuss, (2) obtain form XYZ and have it signed by the supervisor with supporting attachments, (3) supervisor must obtain approvals from certain department heads, etc.
- **Work rule**—These rules stand as a guide for clear action to be taken or not taken in a specific situation. These rules are usually black and white, designed to leave no room for ambiguity or interpretation. For example, "Educational reimbursement will be granted only if an employee takes a class at a college accredited by the following institutions…"

Escalating corrective actions are measures taken by an employer, usually a manager, to fix a problem or wrongdoing that an employee is continually repeating even after initial interventions are taken, such as a verbal and/or written warning. An employee issue can be behavioral or can involve any other aspect of their work that impacts performance. When initial interventions do not produce the desired results, escalating corrective actions need to be taken. Employers may document these specific measures in their employee handbook, or they can be unique, and consequences may need to be altered slightly. Also, in the case of a union environment, there may be very specific disciplinary actions that contractually must be adhered to because they are specified in the collective bargaining agreement. Escalating corrective actions is a logical sequence of discipline that could include required training, suspensions with or without pay, demotions, and sometimes termination. The following is an example of escalating corrective actions:

- Verbal warning
- Written warning
- Mandatory training (if applicable)
- One-day suspension
- One-week suspension
- Two-week suspension
- Termination

Every step needs to be documented: what was incorrect or unacceptable, the expected behavior or performance measure going forward, the discipline being dispensed, and consequences if the corrective actions are not taken.

A **warning** is usually a clear indication that a supervisor or the management team is dissatisfied with an employee's work or attitude. A warning is typically the first step in a progressive discipline process, with the goal being to correct the undesired action(s). A warning can be either verbal or in writing.

- **Verbal**—A verbal warning could be an informal discussion with the employee about their undesired actions and what should be done to improve. It is important that the employee leave the conversation with a clear understanding of the corrective action that must be taken, and what could happen next if the action is not corrected.
- **Written**—A written warning is similar in tone to a verbal warning, except the manager delivers a document or letter detailing the issue with an employee's actions or attitude, and clear expectations about what specifically needs to be corrected. A written warning will also document possible consequences if the issue is not corrected.

Wrongful termination occurs when an employee is illegally terminated from employment, or fired in such a way as to violate an agreed-upon contract or public policy. Laws can vary enormously from state to state on criteria for wrongful termination. The following are some more specific reasons a termination could be wrongful:

- Discrimination
- The employer asking the employee to pursue an illegal act
- Breach of contract
- Termination for whistleblowing
- Violation of company policy

There is not a particular law or regulation that specifically shields or protects an employee against wrongful termination; rather, it is usually other laws, such as anti-discrimination laws, whistleblower protections, public policy, or collective bargaining agreement laws. The majority of states recognize some form of at-will employment, meaning the employer does not need a reason to fire an employee, and an employee is permitted to leave employment without reason or notice. However, the employer cannot terminate an employee in a manner that breaks a law or violates the company's own policies. And just because an employer can fire an employee without reason does not mean that they should do so.

Termination is when an employee is removed from their job. It is often described as a separation from employment. Involuntary termination can result from the employee's failure to abide by the progressive discipline plan due to poor performance or behavior, or from a policy violation. Usually, it is preferable for an employee to know well in advance that continued actions which remain uncorrected could result in termination. Managers should ensure employees understand the gravity and consequences of failure to correct wrongdoing.

If a decision is made to terminate an employee, it should be done swiftly, and employers should take necessary measures to make sure managers understand that departing employees must be treated with dignity and respect during the termination process. Typically, a private meeting is held between the manager, an HR representative, and the employee. The manager delivering the termination should get right to the point and be clear, yet remain sympathetic and patient. Additionally, at the termination meeting, the manager or HR representative should be prepared to discuss the employee's last paycheck and any other financial matters that need to be settled. Final pay and other financial matters are sometimes dictated by state law and regulations. As always, employers should adhere to all federal, state, and local laws and regulations when terminating an employee.

Define the term "offboarding" and explain why it is important.

Detail some of the steps that might be included in an organization's offboarding process.

Explain the importance of retention strategies and how to calculate retention rates.

Define HR policies and procedures and explain why they are necessary.

Describe workplace monitoring parameters.

Describe the basic process of investigating employee misconduct.

Employers' offboarding processes can differ depending on the organization and functions of a job. The following are some of the items that might be included in the offboarding process:

- Planning for the transfer of knowledge from the departing employee to their replacement (if appropriate)
- Reviewing final pay, benefits, and financial information, including retirement options, unused vacation, health coverage, and COBRA (if applicable)
- Collecting all computer equipment, phone, and other technology-related items
- Collecting other employer-issued items, such as uniforms, credit card, and automobile
- Collecting physical keys and security badges
- Deactivating access to company intranet and other systems (email, databases, etc.), as well as related rights and passwords
- Verifying accurate contact information—mailing address, phone number, and email address
- Conducting an exit interview—Usually done by an HR representative to understand the employee's viewpoint on their overall work experience and other concerns that will enable the organization to improve going forward

The terms "onboarding" and "offboarding" evoke images of getting on and off a vessel for an ocean voyage. Employment is being compared to a journey on the ocean. The complexity of the voyage dictates the steps needed for the onboarding and offboarding processes. The same holds true for employment. Every organization wants the beginning and ending of employment to be a good experience. **Offboarding** is a process that includes all decisions and steps that need to be completed when an employee separates from an organization. Offboarding is also an opportunity to talk with an exiting employee about ways to improve the organization. It is important to remember that, when an employee leaves an organization, he or she could be a loyal supporter of the organization, or could speak negatively about the employer. Offboarding gives an employer one final opportunity to influence how the employee feels when they leave. A good offboarding process can help minimize the chance that potential ill feelings might linger. Offboarding leaves a lasting impression in the minds of employees separating from an employer.

An **HR policy** is a set of rules that all members of an organization are required to follow, whereas an **HR procedure** covers the steps necessary to implement a policy. Basically, policy states what rules must be followed in an organization, while procedures detail in writing how to adhere to organizational policies. For an organization to be successful, HR policies and procedures should contain the following core elements:

- Employee role descriptions that detail employee expectations specific to each position in an organization
- Rules and regulations that specify what employees can or cannot do, as well as behavior that is or is not acceptable
- A clear description of consequences for unethical or inappropriate behavior or actions

There are many reasons why an organization needs to have HR policies: (1) They give people defined rules to achieve a respectful environment, (2) they reduce conflict and provide an organization with a certain standard to guide acceptable behavior, and (3) they assist an organization in forming an image in the community that is also helpful for recruiting.

Retention describes the ability of an organization to keep individuals employed within the company. Retention is directly related to the strategies employed by organizations to increase employee engagement and organizational loyalty. These strategies can include competitive compensation strategies, flexibility (e.g., hybrid schedules, working from home, and split shifts), employee recognition and reward programs, positive culture, regular and meaningful feedback, and professional development and advancement opportunities.

Organizations that lack adequate retention strategies—or that have lower levels of engagement and morale—can risk losing members of the organization, including high-potential or top-performing employees. Low retention rates lead to increased recruitment and onboarding costs. Low retention rates can impact organizations from the perspective of the customer and vendor as well. If these individuals deal with a revolving door of contacts, this can cause a loss of trust.

Measuring retention rates and implementing retention strategies will assist the organization with morale, productivity, and consistency. Higher retention rates naturally lead to less turnover. This in turn mitigates the poor morale and poor productivity that likely would have resulted from higher turnover rates. Satisfactory levels of employee retention are critical to organizational success because team building, cohesion, and institutional knowledge come with stability and consistency.

Retention can be calculated using the following formula:

$$\frac{ending\ head\ count\ for\ period}{starting\ head\ count\ for\ period} \times 100$$

The investigation process usually begins when a complaint is received, or when it is determined there is reasonable cause to investigate an employee's conduct. The organization should identify exactly what is being investigated, what sort of evidence is needed to prove or disprove the misconduct, who should be interviewed during the investigation, and which questions need to be asked to gather the necessary evidence. Next, the organization needs to interview the person making the complaint, the individual the complaint is against, and any other employees who have relevant information. Finally, the organization should come to a decision and take appropriate action.

Workplace monitoring is a documented policy and program that an employer can use to monitor and gather information related to suspicious activity by a person in their organization. This monitoring is conducted if the employer has reason to believe a person in their organization is engaged in some activity that might threaten the interests of the business. Monitoring methods might include reviewing internet content usage, wiretapping, GPS tracking, and interviewing other employees. Many of these surveillance methods are easier if the company requires employees to utilize company-issued phones and computers.

Before any workplace monitoring activities are deployed, two actions must occur: (1) employers must be aware of and adhere to all local, state, and federal laws regarding the desired method of workplace monitoring; and (2) employers must ensure that all employees have been made aware and given documentation of all company rules and regulations at the onset of employment, and changes thereafter. Employees' knowledge of employer rules and regulations is helpful if there is unethical or illegal activity because, when such activity is committed, existing employee knowledge proves the activity was committed intentionally by the employee.

Describe Weingarten rights.

Discuss grievances and how they are resolved.

Summarize how discrimination complaints are resolved.

Explain front pay and when it is awarded.

Summarize the basics of the mediation process.

Describe the different types of arbitration.

A **grievance** is a work-related complaint or formal dispute that is brought to the attention of management. However, in nonunion environments, grievances may encompass any discontent or sense of injustice. Grievance procedures provide an orderly and methodical process for hearing and evaluating employee complaints, and they tend to be more developed in unionized companies than in nonunionized companies as a result of labor agreement specifications. These procedures protect employee rights and eliminate the need for strikes or slowdowns every time there is a disagreement.

Disagreements may be unavoidable in situations where the labor contract is open to interpretation because negotiators cannot anticipate all potential conflicts. Formal grievance procedures increase upward communication in organizations and make top management decisions more sensitive to employee emotions. The first step to resolving grievances is for a complaint to be submitted to the supervisor or written and submitted to the union steward.

If these parties cannot find a resolution from there, the complaint may be heard by the superintendent or plant manager and the industrial relations manager. If the union is still unsatisfied, the grievance can be appealed to the next step, which may be arbitration if the company is small. Large corporations may have grievance committees, corporate officers, and/or international union representatives who will meet and hear grievances. However, the final step of an unresolved dispute will be binding arbitration by an outside third party, where both parties come to an acceptable agreement.

In *National Labor Relations Board v. Weingarten*, the Supreme Court established the right of employees to have union representation at investigatory interviews in which the employee must defend conduct or behavior. If an employee believes that discipline or other consequences might follow, he or she has the right to request union representation. However, management does not need to inform an employee of their Weingarten rights. It is the employee's own responsibility to know these rights and request representation. When requested, management can (1) stop questioning until a representative arrives, (2) terminate the interview, or (3) ask the employee to voluntarily relinquish their rights to representation. The company does need to inform the representative of the interview topic, and the representative does have the right to counsel the employee in private and advise them what to say.

When an employer is found guilty of discrimination, the employee who brought forth the complaint is usually permitted to return to their position in the organization. However, the court will sometimes instead rule for front pay. **Front pay** is money awarded to the employee from the employer in a discrimination situation. Generally, the amount awarded is equal to lost wages. There are three situations in which front pay is required from the employer:

- The position left vacant by the employee discriminated against is no longer available.
- The employer has taken no action to rectify the discriminatory practice(s) occurring within the organization.
- The returning employee could be facing an unreasonable, possibly hostile, work environment if he or she were to return to the prior position.

Resolving discrimination complaints requires an employer to decide between two different paths:

- An employer can follow the process defined by the Equal Employment Opportunity Commission (EEOC) and thus be subject to further investigation by the state or local Fair Employment Practice Agency (FEPA). An employee has 180 days from the date of the incident to file a discrimination complaint with the EEOC. After an investigation, probable cause will or will not be found, and the process can go one of two ways:
  - Probable cause found—The EEOC will try conciliation, and the employer can agree to settle, or litigation could be pursued with the EEOC or private court.
  - Probable cause not found—After the 180-day period is over, the employee can ask for a right-to-sue letter, and then has 90 days to file in court. At this point, the EEOC's involvement with the matter ends.
- An employer can make the decision to settle the alleged charges instead of facing an investigation by FEPA.

An employer must contemplate a number of issues before deciding which path is best. Typically, employers will weigh the costs involved in a one-time settlement versus a possibly extended period of legal disruption that could cost both time and money. An open investigation could harm a company's reputation whether the allegations are true or not. Also, if a company believes the claim of discrimination might be truthful, the one-time settlement might make sense in order to quickly pivot, address, and rectify any possible systemic discriminatory practices within the company.

Arbitration is a formal way to settle disputes outside of court. Frequently, parties in a dispute try arbitration if mediation does not work. Parties must agree on a neutral, third-party arbitrator, who listens and makes decisions based on the information and facts presented during the questioning and subsequent discussions. There are many types of arbitration:

- **Binding** arbitration—During this type of arbitration, both parties are required to abide by the final judgment. In other words, the party that "loses" the arbitration must carry out the final judgment. Also, in binding arbitration, this is the end of the legal process: both parties have no other legal recourse with regard to the dispute after a decision is rendered in binding arbitration.
- **Non-binding** arbitration—This type follows the same process as binding arbitration, except the decision rendered does not have to be followed and cannot legally be enforced. Additionally, if either party chooses, they can pursue further legal action.
- **Compulsory** arbitration—In this situation, both parties are required by law to enter into the arbitration process. Generally, this occurs due to one of two reasons: (1) a court order dictated that compulsory arbitration is mandatory, or (2) an agreed-upon contract states that disputes require compulsory arbitration to be resolved.
- **Voluntary** arbitration—The parties in dispute mutually agree to willingly participate in the arbitration process in the hopes of avoiding potentially expensive and time-consuming legal alternatives.

The goal of the **mediation process** is to solve a dispute without having to take more aggressive legal steps. A mediator is specially trained to work with two or more disagreeing parties to reach an agreeable resolution. There is a difference between mediation and arbitration. Arbitration can be the final judgment for a dispute, meaning that if mediation doesn't work, the parties involved can move to arbitration or litigation. Mediation is considered non-binding.

Typically, both parties must mutually agree on a mediator to start the process. A mediator speaks with both parties and there are agreed-upon ground rules, such as logistics, when the negotiation will occur, what specifically will be discussed, who should be involved, and protocol or procedures for discussion. During the agreed-upon negotiations, the mediator will work with both parties to problem-solve and create a reasonable solution to move forward. Frequently, this requires compromise on both sides. If a resolution or compromise is agreed upon, both parties must sign documentation stating they will abide by the agreed-upon plan. If a resolution is not reached during the mediation process, then the parties can either pursue arbitration or litigation to resolve the dispute.

Explain the differences between the types of arbitrators.

Describe some of the methods used to address discrimination, harassment, or bullying.

Explain retaliation in the workplace and how to address this issue.

Summarize the importance of documentation in HR.

Describe why confidentiality is important in the workplace.

Explain what corporate social responsibility (CSR) means and how it impacts an organization's overall strategic direction.

Employees need to know what to do when discrimination, harassment, or bullying occurs in the workplace. There are several ways to address these types of issues. If the employee is comfortable, he or she can confront the perpetrator of the behavior directly. The employee can talk with the perpetrator and let that individual know which behaviors, language, or actions are causing the issue. Individuals can be less defensive when addressed about a possible issue privately. If the concerning behavior, commentary, or actions continue, escalation will be required. Escalation involves bringing the complaint or issue to the next level up. If confronting the perpetrator directly is not successful, the individual can bring the complaint to a team lead, supervisor, or manager. This allows an outside party with a particular level of authority the opportunity to help work through the issue. The leader can mediate between the two parties or address the perpetrator directly. If the behavior persists after escalating to a leader within the organization, or the leader fails to address the complaint satisfactorily, the individual can then escalate the complaint to HR. HR is required to address and investigate complaints of harassment, bullying, or discrimination. HR should meet with the individual raising the complaint to get as much information as possible. HR should also meet with anyone who may have seen or overheard, or has knowledge of, the concerns raised. The person responsible for the areas of concern should also be interviewed. Once the interviews or conversations are complete, the HR department should review all company policies and regulations, as well as employment laws, to determine whether a violation has taken place. If a violation is found, it should be handled according to policy and law. If the concerning behavior persists after HR intervention, if retaliation occurs, or if HR fails to adequately address the issue, the next step in escalation is to lodge a complaint with the EEOC and allow that process to begin. Organizational policies surrounding harassment, bullying, and discrimination should clearly state the levels of escalation so that all employees know what to do should they find themselves in that situation.

There are three different types of arbitrators that could lead the resolution of a dispute. Which type of arbitrator an organization chooses is dependent on the circumstances and previously agreed-upon contracts, if applicable.

- **Permanent** arbitrator—This type of arbitrator usually judges cases for a particular organization or during the life of a contract. In either case, the arbitrator has intimate knowledge of the organization and material being discussed. This knowledge makes arbitration highly efficient, but it is important that both parties continue to believe the arbitrator is unbiased.
- **Ad hoc** arbitrator—In this situation, an arbitrator is mutually agreed upon by both parties, but the arbitrator does not have a previously established relationship with either party. Usually, an ad hoc arbitrator is chosen in one-time situations.
- Arbitrator **panel**—This group of arbitrators, usually three, is similar to ad hoc arbitrators in that they do not have a previously established relationship with the parties involved. This type of panel is sometimes referred to as an arbitral tribunal or a tripartite panel. In the case of a tripartite arbitration panel, the representation is as follows: one arbitrator represents the management, one arbitrator represents the union, and one is neutral. In most cases, the neutral arbitrator is the one who makes the deciding vote.

Documentation in HR is critical, as proper and detailed documentation keeps the organization compliant and protected from questionable lawsuits and legal actions. There must be a clear and consistent documentation process for all HR departments. In the event of official complaints and allegations, those interactions must be written down. Official conversations or interviews related to the complaints must also be documented. When complaints are substantiated, those results need to be written down as well, along with which regulations, policies, or laws were violated. Official counseling, warnings, or disciplinary actions stemming from complaints or concerns should also be recorded. All documents surrounding the complaint should be stored in a central location. This could be in the personnel file or in a separate area for complaints. There are many different templates for investigations, complaints, and employee contact available for use. Thorough documentation illustrates the process and intent behind different actions and can be used to provide evidence for both progressive discipline and termination actions.

Within an organizational setting, retaliation can take place when an employer takes adverse action against advocation of protected rights. Retaliation is usually seen on an individual level. The action taken by the employer could come from an administrator, team lead, supervisor, or manager. Adverse actions can include demoting the employee, passing him or her over for a promotion, excluding that employee from meetings or events, giving unwarranted and excessive negative reviews, transferring the employee to a lesser position, harassing the employee, or even terminating the employee.

Retaliation in the form of adverse actions can result when an employee communicates with an individual of authority within the organization about harassment or discrimination, resists sexual advances, requests a religious or disability accommodation, or refuses to follow directives that could result in some type of discrimination. Retaliation stemming from an employee exercising his or her rights within the workplace is prohibited under law.

When an employee feels that the employer utilized retaliatory acts, he or she can file a charge with the EEOC for investigation. Should the EEOC validate the charge, the employee may receive money for damages (such as a settlement, backpay, or reinstatement to a position) from the employer. Additionally, the employer might be required to change policies and procedures, to complete training, or to take other measures to prevent further issues.

Corporate social responsibility (CSR) refers to an organization's effort to improve its environmental and social impact on the community at large. This is based on the premise that organizations can make the community (and the world) a better place. At the very least, the goal of CSR is to avoid causing damage that will ultimately harm the community. Typically, CSR programs can benefit the organization and its shareholders. Examples of CSR initiatives include, but are not limited to, donating to local charities such as soup kitchens, offering job training or mentoring programs for disadvantaged populations, reducing the organization's negative footprint on the environment, and helping in the event of natural or human-caused disasters.

There is evidence supporting the idea that CSR programs can benefit the organization financially, as well as establishing the organization as a reliable, upstanding member of the community. From an HR perspective, CSR programs could assist in recruiting, as potential employees may seek to work for a socially responsible company. CSR programs may also improve customer relations, brand management, and public relations, which may lead to competitive advantages and the possibility of improved profits.

Confidentiality is vital in HR practices. Maintaining the confidentiality of all employee records is imperative. Information to be safeguarded includes, but is not limited to, Social Security numbers, birth dates, addresses, phone numbers, personal emails, benefits enrollments, medical or other leave details, garnishments, bank account information, disciplinary actions, grievances, and employment eligibility data. When employee record information is requested for legitimate purposes, a written release signed by the employee should be obtained and kept on file. Examples of these requests include employment verification for bank loans and mortgage applications.

Further, HR should internally disclose this sensitive data only to those who are authorized and have a need to know based on the scenario at hand. For example, a supervisor should know employees' disciplinary histories so that they can manage them more effectively. But that supervisor doesn't need to know what benefit plan the employee chose, or that the employee has a tax lien.

However, HR cannot always promise complete confidentiality. For example, if an employee makes a harassment allegation, HR will move to investigate immediately. HR should inform the complainant, and anyone involved in the investigation, that the situation will be handled as discreetly as possible; the nature of an investigation dictates that information obtained during the process may be shared with those who need to know, including the accused.

Describe frameworks to consider when determining whether an organization meets corporate social responsibility (CSR) initiatives.

Explain cultural sensitivity and its importance.

Name some approaches to an inclusive workplace.

Describe diversity and inclusion training.

Describe some ways to advocate for a diverse and inclusive workplace.

Explain how HR practitioners can prepare for operating in a diverse workplace.

Cultural sensitivity can also be referred to as cultural awareness. Cultural sensitivity occurs when individuals understand that people come from a myriad of diverse cultures and backgrounds. Developing cultural sensitivity and acceptance requires individuals to reflect on and identify their own beliefs, values, attitudes, and behaviors that are specific to their own culture. The next step is for individuals to identify values, attitudes, beliefs, and behaviors of other cultures, aimed at gaining a deeper understanding and acceptance of diverse cultures. Differences are recognized, but no one culture is given specific value. One is not better than another; they are simply different. Cultural sensitivity and acceptance require individuals to recognize that not all experiences are shared; in fact, people's experiences differ based on their own upbringing, background, and culture. These experiences can impact both the way an individual interprets information and actions, and how he or she behaves in various instances.

In a professional setting, cultural sensitivity and acceptance are crucial for employees, especially those working on diverse teams. These practices allow communication to not only be effective, but flourish, and will promote an inclusive setting. Cultural sensitivity and acceptance are also important for relationships and exchanges with vendors and business partners. Organizations or individuals who lack cultural sensitivity and acceptance can cause customers, vendors, and partners to feel uncomfortable, marginalized, or disrespected, which could negatively impact the organization.

CSR initiatives often focus on the external community of an organization, while diversity, equity, and inclusion (DEI) is more internally focused. However, CSR initiatives and DEI are closely related, reinforcing one another, and they can be combined to create an even more engaged and motivated workforce. These two areas can be merged to address both internal and external needs. Organizations can review existing company initiatives to determine whether CSR initiatives capture the diverse and varied perspectives of stakeholders. Do existing CSR initiatives leverage the traits, skills, and contributions that make the organization and the surrounding community unique? Does the organization support disadvantaged or underrepresented groups? Do organizational CSR initiatives help redistribute power in tangible ways? How do organizational behaviors and programs promote values and behaviors that make stakeholders feel like members of the community? How does the organization include unique and diverse points of view when developing CSR initiatives?

These are all important frames to review when looking over CSR implementations. Ways to ensure a blending of CSR and DEI can include utilizing diverse suppliers, such as minority- or women-owned businesses. This particular framework is even more successful if small and locally owned organizations are used as suppliers. When researching outside vendors, suppliers, and resources, the organization should investigate where the company is from, what their labor practices are, and what their employee population looks like. Doing business with other organizations that support women and minorities, do not practice unfair labor standards, and do not directly or indirectly promote questionable activity, is a statement in itself and can help the organization build a reputation and commitment as a group that values DEI and CSR.

Although people most often think of diversity as being inclusive of minorities, diversity may also embrace a robust variety of traits such as generation, gender, sexual orientation, race, ethnicity, language, religious background, education, or life experiences. Diversity is the ability to consider and value the perspectives of all people. It is important for HR practitioners to recognize that everyone has both conscious and unconscious biases. **Diversity and inclusion training** supports establishing a nonjudgmental and collaborative workforce that is respectful and sensitive to differences among peers. Additionally, it can teach humility and self-awareness. Training program methods may be extensive or may address specific gaps. Moreover, diversity and inclusion training may introduce new perspectives to the workforce, promoting creativity and innovation.

The first step toward establishing an inclusive workplace is to identify any areas of concern. An internal workforce should reflect the available labor market. Examine the corporate culture and communications to ensure that they advocate for a diverse and inclusive workplace. Review or amend policies and practices to support an inclusive culture. Focus on the behavioral aspects of how people communicate and work together. Are all perspectives respected and input from all positions valued? Address any areas that might not welcome protected classes or disabilities. Then brainstorm approaches and ideas for an inclusive workplace.

Once a diverse culture is established, target recruiting efforts to reach a broad audience. Some ideas may include college recruiting, training centers, career fairs, veteran's offices, and state unemployment offices or career centers. Set business objectives for areas that can be improved upon, document what changes will be implemented, and review progress.

HR practitioners should identify whether there are any areas of concern or need in the organization. Do current employees fairly represent the available talent pool? HR should work to address any unconscious biases or prevailing attitudes in policies or practices that do not support diversity initiatives. They can further support diversity by drawing attention to and eliminating discriminatory perspectives or prejudices. They should train managers on how to fairly and consistently conduct interviews and how to supervise employees from various backgrounds. Moreover, providing appropriate accommodations to employees in need can increase safety, efficiency, and team morale.

Diversity fosters the potential for more perspectives, creative ideas, and innovation. **Inclusion** involves realizing and accepting the benefits and competitive advantages to be had when everyone feels welcome and respected. This environment can be developed with openness, cultural sensitivity, and equal support. HR practitioners can advocate for a diverse and inclusive workplace by reflecting how it can align with business objectives. Building diverse teams can improve problem-solving and productivity and may increase customer satisfaction by providing better representation of an employer's stakeholders. Once buy-in has been gained from upper management, a diversity committee can collaborate to design and communicate initiatives.

Describe different biases and how to avoid them.

Describe different stereotypes and how to avoid them.

Summarize how an HR professional can assist an organization to abide by legal regulations in the workplace.

Explain these three major legal employment regulations overseen by the U.S. Department of Labor: Fair Labors Standards Act, Family Medical Leave Act, and Occupational Safety and Health Act.

Identify and explain key antidiscrimination laws governing how an organization operates.

Explain the purpose of the Equal Employment Opportunity Commission (EEOC).

Stereotypes are overgeneralized, exaggerated, fixed beliefs about a person or a group of people. Stereotypes do not account for individual differences and are used to make assumptions about individuals or groups. These beliefs can be based on traits like sexual orientation, religion, race, gender, ethnicity, education, background, or age. Stereotypes can also form as a result of past experiences. Stereotypes are harmful because they can lead to overt discrimination or more subtle unconscious bias, either of which can, in turn, marginalize certain individuals or groups of people.

Stereotypes exist in all areas of life, including in the workplace. An example of workplace stereotypes could be the belief that women are not able to perform the same roles as men. A woman might be passed over as a machine operator because she is viewed as less physically able than a man might be. Or a woman might be passed over for a promotion, because she isn't viewed as being as competent as a male competitor. Another example is stereotyping based on age. An interviewer may be hesitant to hire an older person, assuming he or she may struggle with technology or may not remain with the organization long due to the proximity of retirement.

Diversity and inclusion initiatives are key to reducing or eliminating stereotyping in the workplace. These initiatives can include DEI training, employee resource groups, and revisions to the interviewing and hiring processes. Individuals can also combat stereotyping by being more self-aware, intentionally collaborating with others from varied backgrounds, and addressing such behaviors and attitudes as they appear.

Bias occurs when a judgment, decision, or assumption is made about an individual or group of individuals based not on objective fact or evidence, but on one's own perceptions and feelings associated with traits such as gender, physical ability, age, sexuality, ethnicity, religion, or race. Unconscious bias, also called implicit bias, occurs when the person making the judgment is unaware of their prejudice.

Unconscious bias can be rooted in learned stereotypes that happen unintentionally or automatically. Unconscious biases can form over time without being detected. They can start as early as childhood and can be learned through environmental and social interactions.

These biases can be present in the workplace and seen throughout the hiring process. For example, when reviewing resumes, a person could reach a conclusion about an individual based only on their name. Another form of unconscious bias seen in the hiring process relates to gender. Individuals may be prone to prefer one gender over the other. To help avoid these biases, it would be beneficial to provide resumes without names or identifying characteristics, instead highlighting skills, experience, qualifications, and education.

To help uncover and eliminate unconscious bias, training and education can be utilized by the organization or the individual. This type of training and education can include teaching individuals how certain factors and behaviors can alienate colleagues, and such education can challenge the individual to recognize prejudices or stereotypes he or she might hold. Incorporating diverse hiring tactics, like resume samples, phone interviews, and standardized questions, can help reduce bias during that process. Organizations should also set hiring goals designed to target diverse individuals, leading to a robust employee pool.

The US Department of Labor (DOL) has established and actively enforces hundreds of employment laws and regulations. The following are three major acts administered by the DOL:

- Fair Labor Standards Act (FLSA)—An act administered by the DOL Wage and Hour Division. Establishes basic wage requirements for employment in the private sector, such as wages, overtime pay, recordkeeping, and employment standards for children.
- Family and Medical Leave Act (FMLA)—An act administered by the DOL Employment Standards Administration. Requires covered employers to provide employees with job protection and unpaid leave in the event of qualified medical and family reasons. Such reasons include pregnancy, adoption, foster care placement of a child, personal or family illness, or family military leave.
- Occupational Safety and Health Act (OSHA)—An act administered by the DOL Occupational Safety and Health Administration. Ensures that employers provide safe and healthy working conditions for employees. Employers covered under the act must comply with legal safety and health standards, ensuring that the workplace is free from hazards.

Compliance with all laws and regulations is mandatory for all aspects of HR programs, practices, and policies. The HR professional must stay current with applicable federal, state, local, and possibly international laws impacting their organization. Basically, HR professionals work to ensure a safe and fair workplace at all times. At the same time, they should also be aware of and ready to communicate the cost of noncompliance with legal regulations, including fines, possible lawsuits, and other liabilities. This means it is necessary to coach managers and employees with regard to applicable laws in such matters as hiring, terminations, and employee relations issues.

HR professionals can assist their employers in hanging legally required posters in common areas, detailing Fair Labor Standards Act (FLSA) and Occupational Safety and Health Act (OSHA) information. The legal requirements for what should be displayed on these posters may differ based on local, state, or federal guidelines. Understanding and complying with all local, state, and federal laws helps the organization and its employees do the right thing and reduce costly legal liability.

The **Equal Employment Opportunity Commission (EEOC)** was formed by Title VII of the Civil Rights Act to protect certain groups of individuals from unlawful discrimination. The EEOC is a federal agency designed to encourage equal employment opportunities; to train employers to avoid practices and policies that could cause unlawful discrimination; and to enforce the laws included in the Civil Rights Act, the Age Discrimination in Employment Act, and laws included in other similar anti-discrimination legislation.

Discriminatory practices by an employer are either intentional (like an employer advertisement saying they will not hire a certain race) or unintentional (such as banning hats for reasons unrelated to safety, being discriminatory against those who wear a head covering for religious purposes). Equal opportunity laws prohibit both intentional and unintentional discrimination. The EEOC attempts to obtain settlements from employers for actions that the commission deems to be discriminatory. If the employer will not settle with the EEOC, the EEOC will continue their attempt to enforce the law by filing a lawsuit against the employer on behalf of the victim of the discrimination.

Employment laws and regulations detail the legal parameters under which an organization must operate. The application of laws may vary depending on the size of an organization, the type of organization, and many other factors. Additionally, requirements can vary based on local, state, and federal laws. A large percentage of employment laws are overseen by the Equal Employment Opportunity Commission (EEOC), a federal government agency that interprets and enforces federal laws prohibiting discrimination.

- Equal Pay Act (EPA) of 1963—Prohibits wage discrimination based on gender for anyone in the same organization, performing the same or a similar job, in the same or similar conditions.
- Title VII of the Civil Rights Act of 1964—Prohibits discrimination based on race, color, religion, gender, or national origin.
- Age Discrimination in Employment Act (ADEA) of 1967—Prohibits discrimination against anyone 40 years of age or older as it relates to hiring, termination, promotion, compensation, and benefits.
- Uniform Guidelines on Employee Selection Procedures (1978)—Procedures that cover all aspects of employee selection decisions (recruiting, testing, interviewing, etc.) designed to achieve equal employment opportunities without any form of discrimination. Note that these are guidelines and not a law.
- Americans with Disabilities Act (ADA) of 1990 and ADA Amendments Act (ADAAA) of 2008—Prohibit discrimination against people with disabilities and guarantee that people with disabilities have the same opportunities as those without disabilities.
- Lilly Ledbetter Fair Pay Act of 2009—Implements a somewhat flexible time frame for filing wage discrimination claims.

Describe EEO reporting.

List the categories EEO reports capture.

Explain EEO-1 reporting.

Discuss the Affordable Care Act (ACA) and regulated reporting requirements.

Explain Title VII of the Civil Rights Act of 1964 and the practices it prohibits.

Identify some of the specific changes the Civil Rights Act of 1991 made to Title VII of the Civil Rights Act of 1964.

EEO reports capture information in nine categories:

- Senior-level officials and managers—Highest-level workers who set strategy, develop policies, and direct.
- Professionals—Jobs that do not always, but usually, require degrees. Includes engineers, accountants, and teachers.
- Technicians—These jobs require very specialized skills for a specific form of work. Includes emergency medical technicians and dental hygienists.
- Sales workers—Workers who list sales as their primary function. Includes retail, real-estate agents, and telemarketers.
- Administrative support—Office and clerical workers. Includes secretaries and payroll clerks.
- Craft workers—Specific skill with advanced knowledge or skills. Includes carpenters, plumbers, and auto mechanics.
- Operatives—Jobs that require minimal training. Operatives are sometimes called semi-skilled. Includes bakers and butchers.
- Laborers—Jobs that require a marginal amount of training. Laborers are referred to as unskilled. Includes assistants and freight movers.
- Service workers—This ranking does not imply that this is the lowest level of work, and some make more money than other categories. Includes janitors, hairstylists, and police.

The **Equal Employment Opportunity (EEO) Act**, passed by Congress in 1972, strives to ensure that any person in the US may not be discriminated against based on age, gender, race, ethnicity, or religion when applying for a job. The EEOC, which enforces the EEO Act, requires annual workforce reporting for any employer with 100 or more employees, and federal contractors who have 50 or more employees as well as contracts of at least $50,000. In addition to reporting, employers must post EEO posters in workplace common spaces in their offices. The reason for the reporting requirement is to calculate and capture the workforce composition and ensure there is no discrimination against a protected class. There are various EEO reports that must be completed if an employer meets the EEO reporting criteria, and none of it is voluntary.

The Affordable Care Act (ACA) requires employers of 50 or more employees to offer healthcare options providing minimum essential coverage that is affordable and gives at least a certain minimum value. This act requires employers with a self-insured health plan to annually complete the following IRS forms:

- **Form 1094-C**—Employer information, including number of full-time employees and total number of employees by month, minimal coverage offered to 95 percent of eligible employees for each month, and whether a 4980H safe harbor (line 16) was used each month.
- **Form 1095-B**—Employee proof of insurance—Employees' share of the lowest-cost monthly premium, and whether a 4980H safe harbor was used each month.

Additionally, employers are required to give a copy of form 1095-B to all employees. Included on this form is information for the IRS and for employees who are covered by the ACA-mandated essential health benefit. Reporting is mandatory for employers with 50 or more (on average) full-time employees. Employers who fail to comply with all ACA requirements and deadlines could be subject to substantial penalties and steep fines.

Private employers with 100 or more employees, and federal contractors with 50 or more employees as well as contracts of at least $50,000, must complete and submit an EEO-1 report each year. This report organizes employee-specific data by race, gender, and job category for an employer. The completed report is submitted to the EEOC and the Office of Federal Contract Compliance Programs (OFCCP) for adherence to federal laws against employment discrimination. This is a mandatory report. If it is not filed, if false information is provided, or if an employer discriminated against an employee, then there are monetary and legal consequences and/or penalties. While there are other EEO reports (EEO-3, EEO-4, EEO-5) that apply to unions, governmental entities, public schools, etc., the EEO-1 report is the reporting mechanism most utilized by the EEOC.

The Civil Rights Act (CRA) of 1991 made the Civil Rights Act of 1964 stronger, but did not replace it. The CRA of 1991 primarily reduced the burden of proof the victim, and made liability for the employer difficult to circumvent, making it easier for employees to sue employers for unlawful discrimination. For example, if an employer is found guilty of intentional unlawful discrimination, the damages awarded to victims could be both compensatory (for emotional distress) and punitive (for breaking the law).

There is a limit on how much juries can award per person. If there are four individuals suing, then the amount awarded increases fourfold. Moreover, the CRA of 1991 offers plaintiffs a jury option in alleged cases of intentional employment discrimination. Prior to the CRA of 1991, the only option was a judge's decision. The CRA of 1991 clarified statutory guidelines for disparate-impact cases (actions that are nondiscriminatory at face value, but negatively impact a member of a protected class under Title VII). Additionally, the CRA of 1991 enhanced the strength of civil rights that were, at the time, losing power by unfavorable Supreme Court decisions, thereby increasing protection for employees from discriminatory treatment.

Title VII of the Civil Rights Act, which was originally passed in 1964 and amended in 1972, 1978, and 1991, is designed to prevent unlawful discrimination in the workplace. This section of the Civil Rights Act makes it unlawful to discriminate against or segregate any aspect of an individual's employment based on any of the following:

- Race
- Color
- National origin
- Religion
- Gender

In other words, Title VII legislation prevents an employer from discriminating with regard to any condition of employment based on these criteria, including recruiting, hiring, and firing. Furthermore, Title VII prohibits an employer from limiting the opportunities for an employee with regard to compensation, career promotions, training, and other employment avenues for advancement or progress. Title VII also makes it unlawful for an employer to discriminate against individuals who are pregnant, are about to give birth, or have any similar medical condition.

Title VII of the Civil Rights Act applies to any employer who has more than 15 employees. Exceptions include religious organizations, which can choose to hire only individuals within that religion, or to consider individuals of that religion for employment before individuals of other religions; and Indian reservations, which can choose to hire or consider Indians living on or near a reservation for employment before other individuals.

Identify which practice the Age Discrimination in Employment Act prohibits.

Describe the Rehabilitation Act of 1973.

Describe the Pregnancy Discrimination Act of 1978 and its protection for child-bearing women.

Identify the practices that the American Disabilities Act (ADA) of 1990 prohibits.

Explain how the ADA Amendments Act (ADAAA) of 2008 amends the American Disabilities Act (ADA) of 1990.

Explain the requirements of the Vietnam Era Veteran's Readjustment Assistance Act (VEVRAA) and who is covered by it.

The **Rehabilitation Act** of 1973 is similar to the Americans with Disabilities Act (ADA) in that the Rehabilitation Act is designed to prevent discrimination against individuals with disabilities. However, the ADA expands the protections granted by the Rehabilitation Act, which was only designed to prevent discrimination against individuals with disabilities if those individuals were seeking employment in federal agencies or with federal contractors that earned more than $10,000 a year from government contracts. Employers were not required under the Rehabilitation Act to make the organization's facilities accessible to individuals with disabilities, so there was no legal remedy for individuals who were employed but unable to access their place of employment.

The Age Discrimination in Employment Act (ADEA), which was originally passed in 1967 and then amended in 1991, is designed to prevent discrimination against individuals over the age of 39. This act makes it unlawful to base decisions related to an individual's employment—such as pay or benefits—on the age of the individual if that individual is at least 40 years old. This act applies to any business, employment agency, labor organization, or state or local government agency with more than 20 employees. Exceptions include individuals age 40 or over who do not meet the occupational qualifications required to perform the tasks reasonably necessary to the business's operations; termination due to reasonable cause; employment of firefighters or police officers; retirement of employees with executive positions; and tenured educators under certain conditions. Pre-employment inquiries about an individual's age are not recommended because it could deter an older worker from applying for a position, and could indicate discriminatory intent by the employer on the basis of age. Someone's age can be determined after the employee is hired.

The **Americans with Disabilities Act** (ADA), which was passed in 1990, is designed to prevent discrimination against individuals with disabilities. A disability, as defined by the ADA, is a mental or physical impairment that impedes one or more life activities. Examples might include, but are not limited to, mobility and personal hygiene. A qualified person with a disability should be able to perform the essential functions of a job with or without reasonable accommodations. This act makes it unlawful to base decisions related to aspects of an individual's employment (such as pay or benefits) on whether the individual is disabled. This act also requires the business, employment agency, or labor organization to ensure the disabled individual has access to his or her place of employment unless making these changes will cause the business significant harm.

There are two main clauses of the **Pregnancy Discrimination Act** (PDA) of 1978. The first clause applies to Title VII's prohibition against sex discrimination, which also directly applies to prejudice on the basis of childbirth, pregnancy, or related medical conditions. The second clause requires that employers treat pregnant women the same as others for all employment-related reasons. In short, the PDA makes it illegal to fire or refuse to hire or promote a woman because she is pregnant; to force a pregnancy leave on women who are willing and able to perform the job; and to stop accruing seniority for a woman because she is out of work to give birth. If a pregnant woman is not able to perform her job because of a medical condition related to the pregnancy, the employer must treat the pregnant woman the same way it treats all other temporary disabilities, which includes providing reasonable accommodations. In addition to the PDA of 1978, employers should be aware of any other state regulations that may afford pregnant women more protections.

The Vietnam Era Veterans' Readjustment Assistance Act (VEVRAA) was designed to prevent discrimination against veterans. Veterans who are protected by VEVRAA fall into four categories:

- Disabled veteran: Entitled to compensation for, or discharged due to, a service-connected disability
- Recently separated veteran: Discharged or released from active duty in the past three years
- Active-duty wartime or campaign badge veteran: Served on active duty during a period of war or during a campaign for which a campaign badge was authorized
- Armed Forces Service Medal veteran: Was awarded (or participated in a military operation for which there was awarded) an Armed Forces Service Medal

Contractors and subcontractors with a single federal contract of at least $200,000 may not discriminate against these qualified protected veterans, and must take affirmative action to employ them and advance them in employment. Companies with more than 50 employees and a single federal contract of at least $200,000 must further have a written affirmative action program.

The **ADA Amendments Act** (ADAAA) of 2008 amends the ADA of 1990 in areas that further clarify protections and definitions of a disability. The following modifications were made in the ADAAA:

- Prohibits the display of so-called "mitigating measures" in assessing whether a person has a disability. Basically, a person will be assessed without certain measures used to manage their impairment, such as prosthetic devices or hearing aids, taken into consideration. Notable exceptions to these measures include eyeglasses and contact lenses.
- Further clarifies the ADA wording of "regarded as" having a disability if employees can prove that they have been discriminated against because of actual or perceived disability. In other words, if employees feel they have been discriminated against for being "regarded as" having a disability and were discriminated against by an employer, the organization could be in violation of the ADAAA of 2008. Note that there could be a true disability or a perceived disability. Examples of discrimination include being denied training or not receiving a promotion.
- Expands the definition of "disability" to include a listing of life activities and conditions, including physical movement, cognitive functions, and medical conditions. The act states that "homosexuality, bisexuality, transvestitism and compulsive gambling" are not considered impairments. In general, most disabling conditions that are temporary in nature are also not included under this act.

Blank card.

Identify practices prohibited by the Immigration Reform and Control Act.

Define an I-9 form and its three parts.

Describe the Vocational Rehabilitation Act and those who are protected.

Explain the purpose of the Uniform Guidelines on Employee Selection Procedures.

Summarize the Genetic Information Non-discrimination Act (GINA) and what protections it affords.

The **Immigration Reform and Control Act** (IRCA) is designed to prevent discrimination based on nationality. This act makes it unlawful for an employer to base employment decisions (such as pay or benefits) on an individual's country of origin or citizenship status, as long as the individual can legally work within the United States. This act also makes it unlawful for an organization to intentionally hire individuals that cannot legally work in the United States and requires completion of the I-9 form for all new employees. This act specifically requires the employer to obtain proof of the employee's eligibility to work in the United States for the I-9 form, but the employee must be allowed to provide any document or combination of documents considered acceptable by the IRCA.

Blank card.

The **Vocational Rehabilitation Act** was intended to increase occupational opportunities for disabled individuals and to prohibit discrimination against qualified individuals with disabilities. In this case, "qualified" means that the person applying for the job can perform the essential function with or without reasonable accommodations. The act applies to federal government contractors and subcontractors holding contracts or subcontracts of $10,000 or more. Contractors and subcontractors with greater than $50,000 in contracts and more than 50 employees must develop written affirmative action plans that address hiring and promoting persons with disabilities.

There are regulations that protect those engaged in addiction treatment; however, this act does not protect individuals who currently suffer from substance abuse that prevents them from performing the duties of the job, or whose employment would constitute a direct threat to the safety and property of others. The primary focus of the act is to extend grants to states for vocational rehabilitation services with a heightened emphasis on those individuals with severe disabilities.

I-9 forms are completed for any employee hired in the United States after November 6, 1986. The form must be completed by the employer, as required by the IRCA, and is used to verify eligibility to work in the U.S.

The I-9 form has three parts:
- Section 1: This section is completed by the employee, and it must be done on the first day of employment. Within the first three days of employment, the employee must prove both identity and eligibility to work in the United States by providing documents that are deemed acceptable as identified on the I-9 form.
- Section 2: This section is completed by the employer (or their representative). The employer must physically examine the employee's acceptable documents and complete the appropriate fields on this section of the form within the first three days of employment.
- Supplement B on the I-9 form should be completed by the employer if a legal name change has occurred, a work authorization has expired, or a previously terminated employee is being rehired.

E-Verify is an electronic/remote internet-based system for confirming employment eligibility.

The **Genetic Information Nondiscrimination Act** (GINA), passed in May 2008, protects people from discrimination based on their genetic information. The act specifically offers protection in two areas: (1) it prohibits discrimination with regard to healthcare coverage based on genetic information, and (2) it protects against discrimination based on genetic information in employment. Employers, under GINA, are not permitted to request any type of genetic information about prospective job candidates or employees, except for a few extreme situations. For example, an employer cannot ask a prospective job candidate about their family medical history. In fact, employers are strongly encouraged to ask healthcare providers not to collect genetic information in the case where an employee needs a medical exam for employment or ADA-related leaves of absence and possible accommodations. Additionally, GINA forbids any type of harassment based on genetic information.

The **Uniform Guidelines on Employee Selection Procedures** (UGESP), passed in 1978, is a procedural document that helps employers to comply with several federal anti-discrimination laws, such as EEO, with an emphasis on Title VII. The primary purpose of these guidelines is to define the specific types of procedures that may cause disparate impact and are considered illegal. These guidelines apply to all aspects of the selection and hiring process: recruiting, interviewing, testing, performance appraisals, and any other factor of consideration used to make employment decisions. The UGESP relates to unfair procedures that make it much less likely that an individual belonging to a protected class would be able to receive a particular position.

Define the term "executive order" and explain the purpose of Executive Order 11246.

Identify and briefly explain some of the executive orders changing the specific groups Executive Order 11246 protected.

Explain affirmative action and what is included in a written affirmative action plan (AAP).

Describe the type of unlawful discrimination known as "disparate impact."

Describe the type of unlawful discrimination known as disparate treatment.

Explain the Copyright Act (Title 17) and related protections.

Originally, Executive Order (EO) 11246 applied only to employment discrimination based on an individual's color, national origin, race, or religion. However, EO 11375, EO 11478, EO 13152, and EO 13279 amended the policy and changed the groups that were covered. EO 11375 made it unlawful to discriminate based on gender, EO 11478 made it unlawful to discriminate based on disabilities or age if that individual is over age 40, EO 13152 made it unlawful to discriminate based on parental status, and EO 13279 excluded federal contractors who were religious and community organizations providing services to the community from the need to adhere to the policies.

An **executive order** is a written declaration made by the president of the United States establishing a policy for enforcing existing legislation. Executive orders are legally binding and are treated as law if the order remains in the Federal Registry for more than 30 days. Executive Order 11246, which was published to the Federal Registry in 1965, states that federal contractors are not only required to avoid employment discrimination but are also required to take steps to ensure equal opportunities are available to individuals belonging to protected classes. This executive order established the concept of affirmative action and required federal contractors with more than $10,000 in government contracts during a single year to implement affirmative action plans, and federal contractors with $50,000 or more in contracts and 50 or more employees to file written affirmative action plans with the Office of Federal Contract Compliance Programs (OFCCP).

Disparate impact is a type of discrimination in which an employer institutes a policy that appears to be reasonable, but prevents individuals of a certain color, national origin, race, religion, or gender, or individuals with certain disabilities or military status, from receiving employment or any of the benefits associated with employment, such as promotions or pay. It refers to a policy that may seem to make sense, but is unfair because it makes things more difficult for individuals of a certain group to receive the job or benefit. For example, a policy stating that individuals applying for an office job must be at least 5'10" and weigh at least 185 pounds may create a disparate impact if it makes it more difficult for women to get the job. However, a physical attribute directly linked to the work that must be performed is not discriminatory so long as it correlates with the essential job requirements. For example, a firefighter has to fulfill certain physical requirements to perform the essential functions of the job. Disparate impact discrimination was first identified by the Supreme Court in *Griggs v. Duke Power Co.*

Affirmative action is a set of written procedures designed to correct discriminatory practices from the past and prevent the continuation of such practices now and in the future. Affirmative action plans (AAPs) were first established by Executive Order 11246, and it is required for those entities doing business with the federal government to have AAPs in compliance with equal employment opportunity laws. In other words, an AAP is supposed to help make sure that every person has equal opportunities when it comes to recruitment, selection, promotion, and training. Moreover, organizations with an AAP must prioritize a quantifiable grouping of qualified candidates who are disabled, minorities, female, and/or covered veterans.

An AAP includes a list of action-oriented programs, an availability analysis of employees from protected classes, a section that designates the individual responsible for the organization's AAP, a job group analysis, an organizational profile, placement goals, a system for internal audits and reports related to analyzing barriers to equal employment opportunities, and a utilization analysis of the number of protected individuals employed by the company compared to the number of protected individuals available. The Office of Federal Contract Compliance Programs (OFCCP) oversees and enforces regulations for those organizations that comply with AAPs. Organizations with AAPs must file their AAP document and report related metrics with the OFCCP annually.

The term **"copyright"** refers to protection from the US government for original works being copied, duplicated, or distributed, and for cases where someone takes credit for someone else's creative expression. **Title 17** of the United States Code includes the **Copyright Act**, first passed in 1976 and amended many times since. The Copyright Act automatically grants protections once the original work is expressed in a medium. In other words, original works are copyright-protected once they are printed, created into an object, in a form of technology, etc. However, it is usually recommended that a person or organization register copyrighted material. To be clear, ideas cannot be copyrighted; rather, it is the tangible expression of the idea in some medium that is copyrighted.

The five primary rights or protections afforded to copyright owners are the ability to authorize others to do the following:
- Reproduce the work
- Distribute the work
- Use the work as a basis for new creations
- Publicly display the work
- Publicly perform the work

The owner of a copyright may be the person who created the work, but if it is a work made for hire, the copyright is given to the person or organization that ordered or commissioned the work. In the commissioned-work scenario, an employer could be the copyright owner.

Disparate treatment is a type of discrimination in which an employer deliberately treats an individual differently because of that individual's age, color, disability, military status, national origin, race, religion, and/or gender. It refers to any instance in which an employer uses a different set of procedures, expectations, or policies than they would normally use simply because the individual belongs to a particular group. For example, a business that requires female employees to follow a strict dress code, while the male employees can wear whatever they like, would be guilty of disparate treatment because of treating employees differently based on gender. In general, an individual claiming disparate treatment must prove that they are a member of a protected class. They must then prove they were qualified but were not hired. If the employer then continues the application process after rejecting a qualified candidate because of a protected class criterion, then this might be considered unlawful discrimination, and thus, disparate treatment. This type of discrimination was first identified by Title VII of the Civil Rights Act.

Summarize the US Patent Act.

Explain the purpose of the Trademark Act.

Summarize employment at will and how it impacts terminations.

List and explain the exceptions to the employment-at-will doctrine.

Define a labor union and its intended purpose.

Summarize collective bargaining and the three discussion topics used in these negotiations.

The **Trademark Act** was passed in 1946 and amended several times. A trademark is any "marking," meaning a logo, slogan, phrase, company name, or combination of attributes, that distinguishes a product or service from others. This distinction enables the product or service to have a competitive advantage in market recognition. In some way, a trademark makes a product or service unique or authentic. The Trademark Act gives certain rights to the owner of the so-called "marking" to prevent other individuals or organizations from using it without authorization. Trademarks, both registered and unregistered with the USPTO, are protected from infringements. In other words, if an organization uses a trademark that is similar to—or likely to be confused with—a widely recognized trademark, it is considered infringement and grounds for legal action.

The **US Patent Act** (Title 35 US Code) grants protection for new inventions whereby no one other than the owner of the patent is allowed to do anything that involves using or selling the invention. Article 1, section 8 of the US Constitution gives Congress the power "to promote the progress of science and useful arts, by securing for limited times to authors and inventors the exclusive right to their respective writings and discoveries." Congress created the United States Patent and Trademark Office (USPTO) to assess and process applications for two types of patents:

- **Utility** patent—This type of patent is issued for inventions that are new and have a use, such as a new machine, process, or manufacturing system. The USPTO qualifies utility patents in five categories: (1) composition of matter, (2) improvement of an existing idea, (3) machine, (4) manufacture, and (5) process. Approximately 90 percent of all patents are utility patents.
- **Design** patent—This type of patent is issued for original designs on an existing product. Sometimes organizations apply for a design patent when the look of a product is changed.

Whoever creates the invention is the owner of the patent. However, if the patent was obtained through work, the inventor often contractually agrees to turn over all rights of the patent to the employer.

There are a few exceptions to employment at will, and they too can vary in execution from state to state:

- **Employment contracts**—If an employee is working under a collective bargaining agreement or other type of specified employment contract, then the employee may have more rights than typical at-will employees.
- **Public policy exception**—Some states prevent an employer from firing an employee in violation of state public policy. For example, in some states with this exception, an employer cannot terminate an employee who was injured on the job and is filing a workers' compensation claim.
- **Implied contracts**—Some states prevent an employer from firing an employee if an implied contract for employment is established between the employer and employee. Cases of implied contracts, where nothing is directly stated or written, are challenging to prove, and the burden rests with the employee. The employee can reference the employer handbook or historical proof that termination is for cause.
- **Good-faith and fair-dealing exception**—Some states specify this exception to prevent an employer from terminating employees to circumvent an employer obligation, such as paying workers for earned commissions, retirement agreements, or healthcare.

The **employment-at-will doctrine** states that an employer can terminate an employee without reason or warning, and also that an employee can choose to resign or leave an organization without reason or warning. An employer's employment-at-will policy should appear in the employee handbook and be clearly communicated to all employees. Additionally, the policy is usually in the contract for employment, if applicable. This type of employer-employee relationship offers ultimate flexibility.

However, it is very important to note that just because an employer or employee can do something—like abruptly terminate an employee or unexpectedly quit a job without notice—does not mean that they should. Wrongful termination in at-will employment situations is protected by federal and state laws, and state laws can vary tremendously. Some of the areas protected in a case of wrongful termination can include termination because of age, gender, sexual orientation, race, religion, disability, or whistleblowing, or termination as retaliation for a legally protected act. All states have some type of at-will employment, but many states place stipulations and limits on how it is interpreted.

Collective bargaining is a process during which unions work to negotiate contracts with employers to help decide the terms and conditions of employment agreements. Employment agreements cover such issues as wages, hours worked, leave policies, health benefits, and conditions of employment such as rules and policies. The National Labor Relations Act has established three types of discussion topics in contract negotiations:

- Mandatory topics, including hours, discipline procedures, wages and overtime pay, processes for firing, layoffs, and reductions in force
- Permitted topics, including how the union board of directors is formed and other matters internal to the union operations
- Illegal topics (topics that cannot be discussed), including unlawful discrimination and unlawful union membership procedures

At the conclusion of the collective bargaining process, the union and the employer reach a collective bargaining agreement (CBA), which is a legal written contract. Both the union and the employer should seek legal advice and counsel, because once the CBA is signed, it is a binding agreement that both parties must abide by.

A **labor union** is a group of workers who organize together as a collective to negotiate with an employer to advance their rights and interests. This negotiation process with an employer is called "collective bargaining." The concept is that a group of individuals banding together is more powerful than a single person fighting for more rights. The formation of unions began in the 1790s and reached its prime in the 1940s and 1950s. Union contracts typically specify safe working conditions, health benefits, compensation in the event of an injury, and retirement stipulations. Additionally, labor unions were extremely influential in ending the practice of child labor. Organized labor unions have diminished since the 1950s, but have meaningfully impacted the economic, political, and workplace environment since their inception. Unions have been partially responsible for a significant amount of federal legislation protecting worker interests and rights, as well as the creation of the US Department of Labor.

Explain the purpose of the Norris-LaGuardia Act and identify some of the specific regulations established.

Discuss some of the employee rights and unfair employer practices outlined in the National Labor Relations Act (NLRA).

Discuss union activities that are prohibited by the Taft-Hartley Act.

Discuss some of the actions controlled by the Landrum-Griffin Act.

Visit *mometrix.com/academy* for a related video.
Enter video code: 972790

Describe the purpose of the National Labor Relations Board (NLRB) and identify some of the specific actions that the NLRB can take to remedy problems caused by unfair labor practices.

Explain the Worker Adjustment and Retraining Notification Act (WARN).

The **National Labor Relations Act** (NLRA) was passed by Congress in 1935 after a long period of conflict in labor relations. Also known as the Wagner Act, after New York Senator Robert Wagner, it was intended to be an economic stabilizer and to establish collective bargaining in industrial relations. Section 7 of the NLRA provides employees with the right to form, join, or assist **labor organizations**, as well as the right to engage in **concerted activities** such as collective bargaining through representatives or other mutual aid. Section 8 of the NLRA also identifies five **unfair labor practices**:

- Employers shall not interfere with or coerce employees away from the rights outlined in Section 7.
- Employers shall not dominate or disrupt the formation of a labor union.
- Employers shall not allow union membership or activity to influence hiring, firing, promotion, or related employment decisions.
- Employers shall not discriminate against or discharge an employee who has given testimony or filed a charge with the NLRA.
- Employers cannot refuse bargaining in good faith with employee representatives.

The **Norris-LaGuardia Act**, which was passed in 1932, protects the right to unionize. This act grants employees the right to form unions and initiate strikes. In addition to granting the right to unionize, this act also prohibits the court system from using injunctions to interfere with any nonviolent union activity and prohibits employers from forcing employees to sign "yellow-dog" contracts. A **yellow-dog contract** refers to any contract that prohibits an employee from joining a union, or any contract that requires an employee to agree to be terminated if it is discovered that they are a member of a union or intend to become a member of a union. The act stated that members belonging to a union have "full freedom of association," meaning they are free to strike, picket, or initiate boycotts without legal penalty.

The government exercised further control over union activities in 1959 by the passage of the Labor Management Reporting and Disclosure Act. More commonly known as the **Landrum-Griffin Act**, this law regulates the **internal conduct of labor unions** to reduce the likelihood of fraud and improper actions. The act imposes controls on five major areas: reports to the secretary of labor, a bill of rights for union members, union trusteeships, conduct of union elections, and financial safeguards. Some key provisions include the following:

- Granting equal rights to every union member with regard to nominations, attending meetings, and voting
- Requiring unions to submit and make available to the public a copy of their constitution, bylaws, and annual financial reports
- Requiring unions to hold regular elections every five years for national organizations and every three years for local organizations
- Monitoring the management and investment of union funds, making embezzlement a federal crime

Because many employers felt that the NLRA gave too much power to unions, Congress passed the Labor Management Relations Act in 1947. More commonly known as the **Taft-Hartley Act**, it sought to avoid unnecessary strikes and impose certain restrictions over union activities. The act addresses **four basic issues**: unfair labor practices by unions, the rights of employees, the rights of employers, and national emergency strikes. Moreover, the act prohibits unions from the following:

- Restraining or coercing employees away from their right to not engage in union activities
- Forcing an employer to discriminate in any way against an employee to encourage or discourage union membership
- Forcing an employer to pay for work or services that are not needed or not performed
- Conducting certain types of strikes or boycotts
- Charging excessive initiation fees or membership dues when employees are required to join a union shop

The **Worker Adjustment and Retraining Notification Act** (WARN), passed in 1988, states that companies must give 60 days' notice in advance of closings and mass layoffs. WARN applies to union and non-union environments, employers with 100 or more full-time employees, or those with total employees cumulatively working 4,000 hours per week at all locations. WARN specifically states that notification must be given to the following: local government, state dislocated worker units, and the workers or their representatives.

There is a difference between a closing and a mass layoff. A closing is a temporary or permanent shutdown of one or more sites or business units at one location in a 30-day period, impacting 50 or more full-time employees. A mass layoff, sometimes called a reduction in force (RIF), is also defined as occurring in a 30-day period, but it is always an employment loss for 50 or more full-time employees, if the layoffs comprise 33 percent of the workforce at the site, or impact 500 or more full-time employees. It is important to note that this is an involuntary employment termination for 6 months or a 50-percent-or-more reduction of hours worked each month for 6 months. There are a few exceptions to the WARN Act, such as natural disasters and "other unforeseeable business circumstances."

The National Labor Relations Board (NLRB) is a federal agency that protects the right of employees to choose whether they want to be represented by a union or not. It is designed to handle activities related to investigating and preventing employers and unions from taking part in unfair labor practices. The NLRB can take a number of actions related to unfair labor practices by employers, including requiring employers to rehire or return positions to employees who were affected by an unfair labor practice, requiring employers to resume negotiations with a union, and disbanding unions that are controlled by an employer. The NLRB may also take a number of actions related to unfair union labor practices, including requiring unions to refund membership fees with or without interest to union members who have been charged unreasonable fees, requiring unions to resume negotiations with an employer, and requiring unions to accept the reinstatement of any employee if the union specifically discriminated against that employee.

Explain the purpose of the Employment Retirement Income Security Act (ERISA) and describe the key provisions.

Detail the three main regulatory obligations employers have under ERISA.

Discuss FLSA and its implications for human resources.

Visit *mometrix.com/academy* for a related video.
Enter video code: 613448

Define an exempt employee and common characteristics.

Provide the three categories that exempt employees may fall into.

Define a nonexempt employee and common characteristics.

The employer has three primary regulatory obligations as it relates to ERISA:

- Obligation to file Form 5500. The IRS, the Department of Labor, and the Pension Benefit Guaranty Corp. developed **Form 5500**, which is for reporting financial conditions, investments, and operations. This form must be completed annually and filed by an employer to satisfy reporting requirements outlined under ERISA and the IRS.
- **Dissemination and disclosure information** for all participants in the employer-sponsored plan.
  - Must have an easily accessible, documented plan
  - Must annually receive a summary plan description (SPD) within 90 days for new participants and 120 days for new plans
  - Must receive (in a timely fashion) a summary material modification (SMM) if the plan is altered no later than 210 days after changes and no later than 60 days if there is a material reduction in coverage
  - Must be given a summary annual report (SAR)
- **Standard of conduct obligation** that requires fiduciaries (trusted individuals) to conduct activities for the sole benefit of the participants and beneficiaries, not in their own self-interest.

If an employer fails to comply with any requirements of this mandate, they could face severe civil and criminal penalties.

The Employee Retirement Income Security Act (ERISA) outlines the standards for private health and pension plans offered by an employer. This act specifies what an employer must do, what they are not permitted to do, and what they might be able to do as it relates to private health and pension plans. This is a complicated statute, but the goal is for employees to receive the benefits promised and outlined by the employer, and to be protected against any type of funds mismanagement.

Most employees who have worked at least 1,000 hours per 12 months, for two consecutive years, are eligible to participate in private pension plans. Employees have the right to receive some portion of employer contributions when their employment ends. Employees must be allowed to transfer pension funds from one retirement account to another. Sufficient funds must be available from the employer to cover future payments. Employers must appoint an individual to be responsible for seeking ideal portfolio options and administering pension funds. Employers must adhere to extensive reporting requirements, provide summary plan documents, and notify participants of any changes. Employers are required to complete annual minimum coverage, actual deferral percentage, actual contribution percentage, and top-heavy testing to prevent discrimination in favor of highly compensated employees. Administration of ERISA is handled by the Department of Labor's Employee Benefits Security Administration, the IRS, and the Pension Benefit Guaranty Corporation.

An **exempt employee** is not entitled to minimum wage or overtime pay as defined by the FLSA. FLSA regulations do not apply to exempt employees. It is usually decided by the employer whether they wish to compensate an employee for working more than 40 hours, and this is usually achieved through bonuses or extra benefits; it is not mandatory. Additionally, exempt employees must meet certain tests based on job duties performed and must earn no less than $684 per week.

It is not job title alone that determines exempt status, but rather the tasks performed on the job.

The **Fair Labor Standards Act of 1938 (FLSA),** also known as the Wage Hour Bill, sets minimum wage standards, overtime pay standards, and child labor restrictions. The act is administered by the Wage and Hour Division of the Department of Labor. The FLSA carefully classifies employees as exempt or nonexempt from provisions, requires that employers calculate overtime for covered employees at one and one-half times the regular rate of pay for all hours worked in excess of 40 hours during a week, and defines how a work week should be measured. The purpose of minimum wage standards is to ensure a living wage and to reduce poverty for low-income families, minority workers, and women. The child labor provisions protect minors from positions that may be harmful to their health or well-being and regulates the hours minors can legally work. The act also outlines requirements for employers to keep records of hours, wages, and related payroll items.

Nonexempt employees fall under the regulation of the FLSA. Nonexempt employees are hourly workers who earn wages less than $684 a week or $35,568 annually. Nonexempt workers must receive at least minimum wage up to 40 hours a week, and must receive overtime pay for any time above 40 hours of work. Overtime pay requires employers to pay at a rate of one and one-half times the employee's regular rate of pay. Generally, nonexempt positions do not require special education, independent judgment or discretion, and/or supervising others; they could work in almost any field. Typically, nonexempt workers have work that is routine and utilizes their body or skills; examples include carpenters, plumbers, craftsmen, mechanics, first responders, park rangers, emergency medical technicians, and correctional officers. Some states have nonexempt regulations in addition to the FLSA.

An exempt employee is paid by salary, not hourly, and spends more than 50 percent of their time performing bona fide exempt functions, usually falling into three general categories:

- Executive employees—Responsibilities include directing the work of two or more full-time employees. The primary focus of their job is management and having direct input into the hiring, ongoing management, and firing of employees.
- Professional employees—This category is most often associated with learned professionals; it requires knowledge and education in a specific field, as with doctors, engineers, and accountants. This category also includes roles in more creative fields that rely on invention, creation, imagination, or artistic talent, such as writers, actors, and graphic designers.
- Administrative employees—Duties include using judgment and discretion with regard to the management of an organization and/or handling high-level interactions with customers.

However, these three categories are not an all-inclusive list; many other types of jobs may be classified as exempt, such as outside sales or computer systems management. Another exempt category could be highly compensated employees, if they do non-manual work, if their salary is $107,432 or higher, and if they also perform work in one of the three main categories. State and local wage and hourly rate laws may have their own requirements in addition to the FLSA.

Explain the characteristics of an independent contractor.

Explain the purpose of the Davis-Bacon Act and the Walsh-Healy Act.

Summarize the Copeland "Anti-kickback" Act.

Describe the minimum wage regulations established by the Fair Labor Standards Act (FLSA).

Identify and briefly explain when it is required to pay an employee more than the federal minimum wage.

Explain the Portal-to-Portal Act and how it impacts compensable time.

The **Davis-Bacon Act**, passed in 1931, requires contractors and subcontractors working on federally funded projects or federally assisted projects—contracted for at least $2,000—to pay wages and fringe benefits at a rate equal to or more than the prevailing wage rates of similar projects in the area. Any employer who performs work to which the Davis-Bacon Act is applicable must place a WH-1321 poster in a workplace common area detailing the wage protections offered by this act. Additionally, employers operating under the Davis-Bacon Act who fail to comply risk losing both their existing federal contracts and their new contract eligibility for three years.

The **Walsh-Healey Act**, passed in 1936, is almost an extension of the Davis-Bacon Act in that the prevailing wage principle was expanded to include manufacturers and suppliers of goods to employers of federal contractors with contracts that exceed $10,000. Furthermore, time-and-one-half wages for nonexempt workers must be paid for any hours over 40 worked in a week. Work sites that must comply with the Walsh-Healey Act are required to post an "Employee Rights on Government Contracts" notice, including wage amount, in a common work area. Similar to the Davis-Bacon Act, penalties for noncompliance are monetarily severe, with the potential for federal contractors to lose their federal contracts and not be eligible to receive new contracts for three years.

An **independent contractor** is not covered by the FLSA and hence not eligible for minimum wage or overtime pay. The most important distinction between an employee and a contractor is whether the worker is dependent on the employer (meaning they are an employee) or conducting business for the sole benefit of himself or herself (making them an independent contractor). The Department of Labor refers to this as an "economic reality test," which takes five factors into consideration:

- Worker's control over the nature of their work, such as schedule, projects, etc.
- Worker's control over profit or loss
- Skill needed by the worker for the work performed, particularly specialized skills that require training
- Worker's relationship with the employer with regard to permanent status
- Whether the worker is part of an existing unit within the organization

The first two factors above carry the most weight and must be examined first. If the worker does have the kind of control described in factors one and two, then there is a substantial likelihood that the worker is an independent contractor. These first two factors are often called "core factors." However, if there is ambiguity, then the next three factors must be examined for clarification. Employers must also comply with all federal, state, and local laws with regard to worker classification, as they may vary.

The FLSA established regulations designed to prevent employees from receiving substandard wages, and it established the minimum wage. The federal minimum wage is the smallest amount an employer can pay for each hour of work; employers must pay at least the amount specified by the federal minimum wage to any nonexempt employee. An employee will be considered exempt from this provision if the individual receives a weekly salary of at least $684, if the employee works in a profession not covered by the FLSA or a profession identified as exempt from the minimum-wage provision of the FLSA, or if the employer has received special permission to pay less than the minimum wage as part of a Department of Labor program.

The Copeland "Anti-Kickback" Act, passed in 1934 and since amended, prevents federal contractors and subcontractors who perform work on covered contracts from persuading an employee to give up any compensation that he or she is rightly entitled to earn based on their contract of employment. All methods of persuasion are prohibited, including force, intimidation, and threat. Prior to the passage of this act, it is estimated that many employees working under a covered federal contract were unfairly intimidated into returning wage earnings to the federal contractor as a so-called "kickback" for employment. There are steep criminal and civil penalties for violating the Copeland Act, including prison time, fines, or both.

The **Portal-to-Portal Act** was passed in 1947 as an amendment to the FLSA to clarify when and under what conditions activities are not considered compensable work time. The general compensation rule is that an employee should be compensated for time worked. This act specified what constituted work time and concluded that activities before work, such as getting ready and commuting, are not compensable. Similarly, activities conducted after work are also not compensable work time. Before- and after-work activities are called "preliminary" and "postliminary" activities.

The Supreme Court interpreted the act to mean that the employer is responsible for compensating employees for activities that are integral and indispensable for principal job functions performed. If a function is integral to the job duties, then the employer must compensate the employee for that work. The following is a non-exhaustive list of situations that would be considered exceptions to the Portal-to-Portal Act, and therefore must be compensated:

- If an employee must travel to various work sites to perform job duties
- If an employee must put on and remove protective clothing for their job
- If a specific type of washing is necessary because an employee is working with toxic or caustic material

There are two situations in which an organization may need to pay an employee more than the federal minimum wage:

- If the individual has worked more than 40 hours in a single week and is in a position covered by the FLSA
- If the minimum wage for the state in which the organization's employees are located is higher than the federal minimum wage

However, most states have their own list of exemptions and requirements, so a particular organization may be part of an industry covered by the FLSA but not by the regulations set by state law.

Describe the Equal Pay Act (EPA).

Explain the purpose of the Retirement Equity Act and identify some of the regulations it established.

Describe the key provisions of the Consolidated Omnibus Budget Reconciliation Act (COBRA).

Discuss some of the main provisions of the Family and Medical Leave Act.

Describe the amendments to Family Medical Leave Act (FMLA).

Discuss the key provisions of the Health Insurance Portability and Accountability Act (HIPAA).

Visit *mometrix.com/academy* for a related video.
Enter video code: 412009

The **Retirement Equity Act** (REA), which was passed in 1984, is an amendment to ERISA designed to establish a number of benefit plan regulations in addition to those originally established by ERISA. These regulations are designed to protect spouses from losing their plan benefits after a plan participant's death or after a divorce, but they also include regulations to strengthen the protections offered by ERISA. Protections established by REA include:

- Regulations prohibiting benefit plan administrators from considering maternity/paternity leave as a break in service regarding the right to participate in a plan or become vested in a plan
- Regulations requiring pension plans to automatically provide benefits to a spouse in the event of the plan participant's death unless a waiver has been signed by both the spouse and the participant
- Regulations that lowered the age at which an employer had to allow an individual to participate in a pension plan

An employer not complying with this act could face severe criminal and civil penalties.

The **Equal Pay Act** (EPA), which was passed in 1963, prevents wage discrimination based on gender. It requires an employer to provide equal pay to men and women performing similar tasks unless the employer can prove that there is an acceptable reason for the difference in pay, such as merit, seniority, or quantity or quality of work performed. This act also establishes the criteria that must be considered to determine whether a particular position is similar or not. This includes the following equal work factors:

- **Skills**—The necessary training, education, and experience needed for a particular position
- **Effort**—This includes the physical and mental capabilities required for a given position
- **Responsibility**—This is primarily an issue of accountability and the degree to which an employer relies on employees to successfully accomplish their job
- **Working conditions**—The physical working environment (e.g., hazardous, indoors, outdoors, cold, hot)

The **Family and Medical Leave Act** (FMLA) of 1993 is a federal regulation that provides employees the right to take up to 12 weeks of unpaid leave in each 12-month period for the care of specified medical conditions that affect themselves or immediate family members. To be eligible for FMLA leave, an employee must have worked for a covered employer for the preceding 12 months and for a minimum of 1,250 hours during that time. All private employers, public or government agencies, and local schools with 50 or more employees within a 75-mile radius, must adhere to the regulations. Qualifying events covered under FMLA include the following:

- The birth or adoption of a new child within one year of birth or placement
- The employee's own serious health condition that involves a period of incapacity
- An ill or injured spouse, child, or parent who requires the employee's care
- Any qualifying exigency due to active-duty foreign deployment by an employee's spouse, child (or children), or parent. Exigencies may include arranging childcare, tending to legal matters, and attending military ceremonies.
- The care of an ill or injured covered service member, as long as the employee is a spouse, child, parent, or next of kin. In addition, time to care for military personnel or recent veterans has been expanded to 26 weeks in a 12-month period.

Additionally, employers covered by FMLA must display a poster in a common area workspace that outlines FMLA provisions, including how to file a complaint.

The **Consolidated Omnibus Budget Reconciliation Act** (COBRA) of 1986 requires that all employers with 20 or more employees continue the availability of healthcare benefits coverage and protect employees from the potential economic hardship of losing these benefits when they are terminated, are working reduced hours, or quit. COBRA also provides coverage to the employee's spouse and dependents as qualified beneficiaries. Events that qualify for this continuation of coverage include the following:

- Voluntary or involuntary termination for any reason other than gross misconduct
- Reduction in hours that would otherwise result in loss of coverage
- Divorce or legal separation from the employee
- Death of the employee
- The employee becoming disabled and entitled to Medicare
- The dependent being over 26 and no longer a dependent child under plan rules

Typically, the employee and qualified beneficiaries are entitled to 18 months of continued coverage. There are some instances that will extend coverage for up to an additional 18 months. Coverage will be lost if the employer terminates group coverage, premium payments are not received, or new coverage becomes available. COBRA is a high-cost plan; typically the cost to the employee is the full cost that the employer pays for health coverage, plus an administrative fee that averages around 2 percent. Alternatives to COBRA are purchasing coverage through marketplace offerings, Medicaid coverage if applicable, or switching coverage through a spouse (again, if applicable) because a qualifying event entitles the spouse to special enrollment.

The **Health Insurance Portability and Accountability Act** (HIPAA) was passed in 1996 to provide greater protections and portability in healthcare coverage. Some individuals felt locked into current employer plans and feared that they would not be able to obtain coverage from a new employer plan due to preexisting conditions. As a result, some of the key HIPAA provisions are pre-existing condition exclusions, pregnancy, newborn and adopted children, credible coverage, renewal of coverage, medical savings accounts, tax benefits, and privacy provisions. Employees who have had another policy for the preceding 12 months cannot be excluded from coverage due to a pre-existing condition or pregnancy, and it must be applied to newborn or adopted children who are covered by credible coverage within 30 days of the event. **Credible coverage** involves being covered under typical group health plans, and this coverage must be renewable to most groups and individuals as long as premiums are paid. **Medical savings accounts** were created by Congress for those who are self-employed or otherwise not eligible for credible coverage. Individuals who are self-employed are also allowed to take 80 percent of health-related expenses as a deduction. Finally, HIPAA introduced a series of several regulations that impose **civil and criminal penalties** on employers who disclose personal health information without consent.

The FMLA has undergone some significant amendments, and HR practitioners should be aware of the following:

- If an organization fails to denote an employee's leave as FMLA leave, the employee may be eligible to receive compensation for any losses incurred.
- Prior to 2008, all FMLA disputes required Department of Labor or legal intervention. Now, employees and employers are encouraged to work out any issues in-house to avoid the cost of litigation.
- Light duty does not count toward FMLA taken.
- FMLA covers medical issues arising from preexisting conditions.
- Due to their unique scheduling, airline employees are eligible for FMLA after 504 or more hours worked during the preceding 12 months.

Explain the purpose and application of the Work Opportunity Tax Credit (WOTC).

Describe provisions of the Uniformed Services Employment and Re-employment Rights Act (USERRA).

Describe the escalator principle of USERRA.

Explain the purpose of the Mental Health Parity Act.

Discuss the Lilly Ledbetter Fair Pay Act of 2009.

Describe the key provisions of the Patient Protection and Affordable Care Act (PPACA).

The **Uniformed Services Employment and Reemployment Rights Act** (USERRA) of 1994 is applicable to all employers, both public and private. USERRA forbids employers from denying employment, reemployment, retention, promotion, or employment benefits due to service in the Armed Forces, Reserves, National Guard, and other uniformed services, including the National Disaster Medical System and the Commissioned Corps of the Public Health Service. In other words, this statute is designed to prevent those in the uniformed services from being discriminated against or otherwise disadvantaged in the civilian workplace because of their military service or affiliation. Employees absent in uniformed services for less than 31 days must report to the employer within 8 hours after arriving safely home. Those who are absent between 31 and 180 days must submit an application for reemployment within 14 days. Those who are absent 181 days or more have 90 days to submit an application for reemployment.

The **Work Opportunity Tax Credit** (WOTC) is a federal tax credit that is provided to employers who hire individuals that are part of targeted groups facing significant challenges or barriers to employment. The tax credit is intended to financially incent employers to hire from these 10 targeted groups:

- Qualified veterans
- Qualified ex-felons
- Designated community residents, meaning individuals living in designated empowerment zones or rural renewal counties
- Vocational rehabilitation referrals
- Summer youth employees living in an empowerment zone
- Supplemental Nutrition Assistance Program (food stamps) recipients
- Supplemental Security Income recipients
- Long-term Temporary Assistance for Needy Families (TANF) recipients
- Qualified long-term unemployment recipients
- Qualified long-term family assistance recipients

There are many stipulations and specific qualifications for all the targeted groups. Generally, the tax credit is based on three factors: the category of the worker, compensation to the employee, and the number of hours they worked. The WOTC is authorized until December 31, 2025 (Section 113 of Division EE of P.L.116-260—Consolidated Appropriations Act, 2021). The Department of Labor (DOL), the Department of the Treasury, and the IRS all play a role in administering the WOTC program with employers.

The **Mental Health Parity and Addiction Equity Act** (MHPAEA), which was passed in 1996, is designed to prevent health plan providers from setting limits on mental health benefits that are stricter than the limits the provider has set for other health benefits. This act prohibits a health plan provider from setting a financial cap on the amount the health plan provider will pay for mental health benefits if that cap is lower than the cap the provider has set for other benefits. For example, if a medical or surgical lifetime cap is $8,000, then the cap on mental health benefits cannot be below $8,000. This act applies to any health plan provider providing coverage for an employer with at least 51 employees, but only if the regulations set by this act will not result in a 1 percent or greater increase in the costs of the provider. Also, health plan providers are not required to offer mental health benefits, and providers may set other limits related to mental health coverage as long as there is no specific payout limit.

Employees are entitled to the positions that they would have held if they had remained continuously employed. If they are no longer qualified for or able to perform the job requirements because of a service-related disability, they are to be provided with a position of equal seniority, status, and pay. Moreover, the escalator principle further entitles returning employees to all of the seniority-based benefits they had when their service began, plus any additional benefits they would have accrued with reasonable certainty if they had remained continuously employed. Likewise, employees cannot be required to use accrued vacation or PTO during absences. USERRA requires all healthcare plans to provide COBRA coverage for up to 18 months of absence and entitles employees to restoration of coverage upon return. Pension plans must remain undisturbed by absences as well. However, those separated from the service for less-than-honorable circumstances are not protected by USERRA.

The **Patient Protection and Affordable Care Act** (PPACA) is a comprehensive healthcare law that was passed in 2010 to establish regulations on medical services, insurance coverage, preventative services, whistleblowing, and similar practices. A few key provisions of the PPACA include the following:

- **Individual mandate**—Requires all individuals to maintain health insurance or pay a penalty. It was removed from the statute effective tax year 2019. However, there are a few states that have an individual mandate.
- **State healthcare exchanges**—Provides individuals and families a portal in which they can shop through a variety of plans and purchase healthcare coverage.
- **Employer shared responsibility**—Requires that employers with more than 50 full-time employees provide affordable coverage to all employees that work 30 or more hours per week or pay a penalty.
- **Affordable coverage**—Does not allow employers to shift the burden of healthcare costs to employees and imposes a penalty on employers if their employees qualify to obtain government subsidies for coverage.

The **Lilly Ledbetter Fair Pay Act** overturned the 2007 Supreme Court decision in the *Ledbetter v. Goodyear Tire & Rubber Company* case, which ruled that the statute of limitations to make a discriminatory pay claim was 180 days from the first discriminatory paycheck. Because of the Lilly Ledbetter Act, the statute of limitations now restarts with each discriminatory paycheck. The act applies to all protected classes and covers both wages and pensions. Due to the scope of the act, employers could face claims years after an employee has left the company. This act was designed to make employers more proactive in resolving pay inequities. Additionally, employers should review their compensation record retention procedures in case they need to produce any related documentation for potential pay disparities.

Describe additional provisions of the Patient Protection and Affordable Care Act (PPACA).

Explain how taxes affect compensation which benefits are considered taxable.

Explain what workplace confidentiality means.

Explain confidentiality rules as they pertain to employee records.

Summarize confidentiality rules as they pertain to company data.

Explain privacy principles and how they might impact the workforce.

There are several things to be aware of when considering the implications of taxes for compensation and benefits. The first area to consider is tax treatment of compensation. Employee gross wages, including overtime, are subject to federal income tax (FIT). In addition, Social Security and Medicare are taxed under the Federal Insurance Contributions Act (FICA). Meanwhile, employers pay federal unemployment insurance (FUTA) taxes.

The second area to consider is tax treatment of benefits. The most common benefits that are not taxable are:
- Commuting/transportation expenses
- Health benefits, including care for dependents
- Most group life insurance plans
- Plans such as 401(k) programs that are considered "qualified benefits plans"

The most common taxable benefits are those that can be considered a form of payment for the performance of a service. The following are subject to FIT, FICA, and FUTA taxes:
- Paid vacations
- Using a company-issued car for commuting to and from the workplace
- Company-paid bonuses
- Gym or health club memberships

- **Flexible spending accounts (FSAs)**—Imposes a cap on pretax contributions to FSAs, health reimbursement arrangements (HRAs), and health savings accounts (HSAs).
- **Wellness incentives**—Allows employers to provide premium discounts for employees who meet wellness requirements.
- **Excise tax on "Cadillac" plans**—Imposes excise tax on employers that provide expensive coverage.
- **W-2 reporting requirements**—Requires employers to report the cost of coverage under employer-sponsored group health plans on each employee's W-2 form.
- **Summary of benefits coverage**—Requires insurance companies and employers to provide individuals with a summary of benefits coverage (SBC) using a standard form.
- **Whistleblower protections**—Amends the FLSA to prohibit employers from retaliating against an employee who applies for health benefit subsidies or tax credits.

An organization's HR department collects a substantial amount of employee paperwork: completed job applications, resumes, contact information, completed benefit forms, performance evaluations, and possibly performance improvement plans and medical records. Some documents, whether in paper or electronic form, must remain private and thus protected. Medical records absolutely must be kept confidential, as release of this information in any form could be a violation of the Americans with Disabilities Act (ADA), the Genetic Information Nondiscrimination Act (GINA), and/or the Health Insurance Portability and Accountability Act (HIPAA).

The rationale for confidentiality is that this type of information, if not held private, could result in possible discriminatory decisions by an organization. For example, the ADA maintains that employee medical information must be kept separate—in a locked file cabinet or secured behind a firewall, for instance—from the employee's personnel record. This is a specific legal ruling. However, there are other documents that most organizations should keep secure and private because it is in everyone's best interest, including I-9 forms, background check results, performance evaluations, termination data, and investigative documents (harassment, complaints, etc.). These documents may include information that could potentially be utilized in a discrimination case against the employer if it is released and wrongdoing is suspected.

Workplace confidentiality is defined as the policies and procedures created by an organization to maintain confidential, private, sensitive, or compromising information related to the employer and its employees. Confidential or private information may include, but is not limited to, business planning and forecasting, client information and contracts, research and development studies, and employee records. HR plays a vital role in maintaining confidential and private information. There are laws for specific types of data and how they should be maintained, and other data types come with suggested procedures to securely protect an organization from legal risks. A general litmus test in the dissemination of private information is:
- Is sharing the information legal?
- Does the individual or group absolutely need to know because their input is mandatory in order to investigate, settle, or solve the issue?

A breach exposing confidential or private information can result in a broad range of negative consequences legally, financially, and in the court of public opinion.

With technology now a part of every business transaction, it is essential that companies and employees adhere to strict confidentiality practices and **privacy principles**. From employee monitoring to asking interview questions, employers need to carefully avoid invading personal privacy. Legal regulations that inform best practices and internal privacy policies should be consulted regularly for guidance. On the other hand, companies should consider implementing confidentiality or nondisclosure agreements so employees are aware that databases, client lists, and other proprietary information must be protected and that the sharing of these records externally is strictly prohibited.

Company data must be kept private and only released to those who have been identified as needing to know the information in order to operate the organization. Typically, the following information is considered proprietary and confidential data: client names, sources of revenue, expenditures and losses, trade secrets, and all business processes and operations. Confidentiality applies to paper and electronic company data. Paper documents must be kept in a secure, locked location, and electronic data must have appropriate firewalls and password protection.

Organizations will often have an employee sign a privacy or nondisclosure agreement that clearly documents what information is protected, and how and with whom proprietary information can be shared. This is an important step to avoid potentially negative legal repercussions, loss of business, or competitive advantage. For example, if an employee reveals trade secrets to a competitor, thus causing harm to their employer, they are in violation of their nondisclosure agreement and could face legal consequences. Additionally, some organizations have procedures in place for protecting intellectual property via trademark, patent, and copyright protocols.

Describe employee monitoring software and how it is used.

Summarize the need for confidentiality disclosures in technology.

Describe the purpose and types of Occupational Safety and Health Act (OSHA) reporting.

Visit *mometrix.com/academy* for a related video.
Enter video code: 913559

Explain the two different types of sexual harassment.

Discuss employer and employee rights in the case of substance abuse.

Discuss some examples of drug and alcohol policies contained in the ADA.

Confidentiality disclosures should include definitions and exclusions of confidential information while outlining individual responsibilities. Confidentiality disclosures are used to keep private or secure information available only to those who are authorized to access it. It is important to ensure that only the proper individuals have access to the information needed to perform their jobs. Moreover, legislation mandates due diligence to protect the confidential information of employees and customers. Technological breaches in confidentiality could happen via phone, fax, computer, email, and electronic records. For this reason, some businesses might utilize encryption software, limit the communications that can be sent via email, or include a statement notifying the reader what to do if the email is inadvertently sent to the wrong person.

An organization may choose to utilize **employee monitoring software** to gain information on how employees are using their time at work. Usually, monitoring software allows the employer to see internet activity and software usage. It can also save random screenshots and track keystrokes. This monitoring is typically done from a central location, but can also capture information from local and remote computers. The rationale behind employee monitoring software is to understand how an employee spends their time while working because it can directly and indirectly impact the organization's productivity and security.

Best practices for the deployment of employee monitoring software includes clearly communicating to employees, usually in an HR handbook or company policy manual, what is and is not appropriate computer usage in a given organization, and possible repercussions for violating such a policy. It is important that the employee know from the beginning of their employment that the organization has the right to monitor all technology use from company-procured or sponsored equipment. The goal is to effectively design and communicate a technology policy that protects the organization from threats such as viruses, hacking, or unethical activity, while at the same time providing employees some balance in internet and/or software usage.

Title VII of the Civil Rights Act of 1964 prohibits sexual harassment. There are two different types of sexual harassment in the workplace: quid pro quo and hostile work environment.
Quid pro quo literally means "this for that." This type of harassment occurs when a supervisor, manager, or someone with authority demands some form of sexual interaction in exchange for an employment-related benefit, such as more compensation, a promotion, or keeping a current job. In other words, the person with authority basically states, "If you do some sexual favor for me, then I will provide some work benefit for you." A worker is then coerced or forced into unwelcome sexual demands to avoid negatively impacting their job.
A hostile work environment occurs when an employee is confronted with unwelcome, sexually offensive conduct that is severe and in a clear, pervasive pattern, thereby creating an abusive environment. Some of the circumstances that should be examined in a possible hostile environment are as follows:
- How often the offensive, discriminatory action occurs
- How severe the actions are
- Whether the conduct can cause or has caused physical harm, is intimidating, or is more subtle
- Whether it unreasonably prevents the employee from performing his or her job
The goal for organizations is to try and prevent sexual harassment. This can be done by clearly communicating the organization's policy that sexual harassment will not be tolerated, and by providing training. However, if sexual harassment occurs, there needs to be a formal complaint process whereby it is immediately investigated, and swift and fair action is taken to stop the harassment.

The Occupational Safety and Health Act (OSHA) of 1970 set safety and related recordkeeping standards for the workplace. Safety records could include a log of occupational injuries and illnesses related to work while performing a job, a record and summaries of illnesses and injuries, and a record of any toxic exposures for employees. OSHA regulations require compliance by an organization that is engaged in commerce and has one or more employees. OSHA also protects employees who may work in substandard conditions by informing them of their rights and providing training to remedy the situation. An employee can reach out to OSHA to investigate possible substandard conditions without legal fear of retaliation. The following are the OSHA forms that an organization may have to complete, depending on the situation.
- Form 300—Used by an employer to record and keep information about an injury or illness an employee experienced. There are three parts to this form: (1) identification, including name of the person, maybe a case number, job title, and department; (2) description of event, with date, location, and summary of event; and (3) classification of injury or illness, its type, number of days off from work, and any restrictions.
- Form 301—Used if the injury or illness event has supplemental material that needs to be documented. For example, it may contain information about events leading up to the occurrence, or whether an object or substance was involved.
- Form 300A—A summary of illnesses and injuries that occurred throughout the year. Form 300A does not contain any of the personal information that is on Form 300. The primary purpose of this form is to calculate incident rates.

It is important to keep in mind that the Americans with Disabilities Act (ADA) and the Rehabilitation Act of 1973 include drug and alcohol policies, and some states have their own policies. The following are some examples to keep in mind:
- The ADA does not prohibit an employer from testing for illegal drug use, although it must follow any applicable state protocols.
- Some states restrict pre-employment drug testing until the candidate has accepted the job. It is usually a good practice to test all candidates instead of singling out any one individual.
- Some states can randomly test workers for drugs, especially where safety is an issue. However, there are also some states where an employer must have a reasonable suspicion before requiring an employee to be drug-tested.
- An employer—if applicable, and if possible—must offer reasonable accommodations for employees with substance abuse problems, in their past or currently, to attend to medical care.
- Under the ADA, a person considered an alcoholic might be considered an "individual with a disability" and treated accordingly.

There are federal and state laws outlining policies an employer can develop to combat drug and alcohol abuse in the workplace. Generally, employers implement three policies that address this type of abuse: (1) unequivocally prohibit alcohol and drug use on the job, (2) provide permission to test for drug use (within guidelines), and (3) fire employees who have been proven to use illegal drugs. Employers should document their drug and alcohol policies, including what could happen if someone fails a drug test. Employees also have some protections afforded to them from both federal and state laws, whereby the employer may have to provide some accommodations to address the substance abuse problem.

Discuss issues with employers and an employee's right to privacy.

Describe the implications of defamation.

Explain the characteristics of fraudulent misrepresentation.

Describe the Drug-Free Workplace Act.

Explain the protections offered by the Sarbanes-Oxley Act (SOX).

Summarize the key elements of workplace records retention management and access.

Defamation is when a person intentionally makes a false and malicious statement causing harm to a person's reputation in a given community. If harm is caused by speaking, it is called slander. If it is in written form, it is called libel. For example, if someone makes a negative statement during a reference check regarding a former employee, or over-the-top positive comments, then the person giving the reference could be liable for making distorted false claims. Another example of this type of misrepresentation could be when an employee is upset because he or she was passed over for a promotion and decides to spread a rumor that the person who received the promotion lied about their qualifications.

The First Amendment, which protects free speech, does not protect someone guilty of defamation, and as a result, the person can face legal consequences. Many companies have implemented policies to try and reduce the likelihood of harmful gossip and rumors that cause needless stress and negatively impact productivity.

There is no specific federal law that compels employers to inform employees about any type of monitoring in the workplace. Therefore, US employers have the right to monitor employees with such things as surveillance cameras, internet tracking, or email or phone tracking applications. The ability to do this is a double-edged sword for employers. Technology affords employers many ways to monitor, which is helpful for reducing liability and perhaps increasing productivity. However, at the same time, employees have almost no choice other than to surrender most of their privacy while at work.

There is much debate among employers about the ethical, moral, and legal decisions to reduce employee privacy rights. There is also the question of where it ends, such as whether an employer should use a candidate's social media presence when making a decision to hire. The debate continues about how a company can strike a balance between employer rights and employee privacy. Every company is different and needs to evaluate whether the monitoring is worth the effort and what the monitoring is doing to drive better business results. Additionally, a company may want to consider how the monitoring will impact its culture: Will employees want to work for a company that aggressively monitors its employees? There are no right or wrong answers, but it is helpful for companies to be clear and transparent about employee privacy and monitoring activities.

The Drug-Free Workplace Act of 1988 requires that government contractors make a good-faith effort to ensure a drug-free workplace. Employers must prohibit illegal substances in the workplace and must create drug awareness trainings for employees. Any federal contractor with contracts of $100,000 or more, and all organizations that are federal grantees, must adhere to a set of mandates to show they maintain a drug-free work environment:

- Employers must develop a written policy prohibiting the production, distribution, use, or possession of any controlled substance by an employee while in the workplace.
- Employers are required to develop standards of enforcement, and all employees must receive a copy of the policy and understand the consequences of a violation.
- Employers need to implement drug awareness trainings to help employees understand the hazards and health risks of drug use.
- Although drug testing is not required, it is intended that employers have some type of screening in place.

Fraudulent misrepresentation is an intentionally false statement that deceptively causes someone to enter into a contract. Basically, someone can be accused of fraudulent misrepresentation if a statement of fact is a blatant lie, and this lie creates a false pretense under which another person enters into a contract. For example, suppose an employer says to a prospective applicant that the company is doing great financially and job security is strong. Hearing this, the applicant turns down other jobs for the one with the most job security. He accepts the position and learns three months later that the company has not been profitable in many months and the employer knew the job would only be temporary without any job security whatsoever. This is a case of fraudulent misrepresentation, in which the job applicant entered into a contract of employment with an expectation of job security when the employer knew that was not true.

Fraudulent misrepresentation can occur in any form that results in the other party being deceived with false information, a half-truth, or silence when there was an opportunity to speak up. Also, fraudulent misrepresentation requires the deceived party to enter into a contract; this is different from defamation, which is when an intentionally false statement is made about a person without the involvement of contracts.

Workplace employee-related records should have organizational policies that might be regulated by federal, state, and local laws as well as operational necessity. It is sometimes easier to think of a record as the complete, final version of a document so that there is no need to keep every draft or note. The following are key elements of workplace records retention management and access:

- How long to **retain** records—First, all records that are regulated by law should be kept for the prescribed time period according to federal, state, and/or local laws. This can be confusing because certain records might be regulated by more than one law, or the time period may vary. In these cases, records should be kept for the longest period required.
- Who should have **access** to records—Access should be provided (1) only to those people with a legitimate business need, and (2) only where federal, state, and local laws permit such access. For example, HIPAA and many data privacy regulations specify not only who may have access, but how the information may be used.

The Sarbanes-Oxley Act (SOX) was passed in 2002 to provide accountability, standards, and oversight to prevent corporate fraud. The act was largely in response to major corporate accounting scandals in the early 21st century like those at WorldCom and Enron. In turn, the passage of SOX created the Public Company Accounting Oversight Board (PCAOB) as an oversight agency for the accounting industry. However, the Securities and Exchange Commission (SEC) enforces compliance with SOX.

SOX holds senior executives responsible for any accounting misconduct or manipulation. Additionally, the law protects shareholders from any activity that might mislead or influence investors about the company's financial health and outlook. Under SOX, a public corporation is required to accurately report financial information to both investors and the SEC. If the information reported to the SEC is later found to be inaccurate or altered in any form, there are large financial penalties and stringent white-collar crime consequences. Additionally, SOX offers protection to whistleblowers who report fraud and could potentially testify against their employer.

Explain how records should be stored and what security is needed to safeguard records.

Explain some concerns an organization should consider before the destruction of HR records.

Summarize what pre-employment records should be retained and why.

Summarize what employment records should be retained, the length of time they should be retained, and why they should be retained.

Summarize what employment records should be retained, the length of time they should be retained, and why they should be retained.

Explain why an organization might separate a personnel file into two categories.

Employee records management is critical to comply with federal, state, and local requirements and to reduce legal liabilities. If an organization prematurely destroys HR records, that organization could face criminal liabilities and possible legal penalties or litigation. Additionally, the organization may not be able to adequately defend itself in employment-related litigation due to spoliation of evidence. An organization should only retain the legal HR records that are required to comply with federal, state, and local laws or operational necessity. For example, holding on to every scrap of paper an employee writes on is not necessary; only legally mandated documents are necessary. In some cases, keeping every scrap could turn into a liability for the organization.

The end goal for HR is to keep what is legally mandated and to properly, legally dispose of the rest. Disposal of confidential, personal, or financial information after the legally dictated retention period is over should comply with all federal, state, and local regulations. For example, the Fair and Accurate Credit Transactions Act (FACTA) has specific rules for how to dispose of background check documentation. Usually, if it is paper, this means shredding on-site or hiring a professional vendor that specializes in shredding. In the case of electronic records, the organization must follow protocols so that the information is erased and cannot be read or reconstructed.

Employee records, whether they are paper or electronic, have specific retention requirements. Retention of employee records could vary according to federal, state, and local laws. Therefore, it is important to understand the legal requirements as well as the system that an organization utilizes. The following is a summary of federal guidelines for the most common HR records.

- **I-9 forms**—Securely retained for three years beginning from the hire date, or one year after separation of employment.
- **Payroll records**—These records, which contain personal information such as name, address, Social Security number, and compensation, should be retained for three years according to federal laws. There are many federal laws that regulate payroll records, including the Age Discrimination Employment Act (ADEA), Fair Labor Standards Act (FLSA), Service Contract Act, Davis-Bacon Act, Walsh-Healey Act (for federal contractors), and Family and Medical Leave Act (FMLA). However, it is recommended for the purposes of the Lilly Ledbetter Fair Pay Act to retain these documents for at least five years after the end of employment. Additionally, under the Equal Pay Act (EPA), employers must retain two years of all payroll records in case they need to justify the pay wage differential between different sexes.
- **Employment benefits**—These records should be retained for six years and are carefully regulated, requiring employer reporting based on the Employee Retirement Income Security Act (ERISA).

Not every record in a personnel file should be treated the same. Specific records regarding an employee and their employment history should be kept in their personnel file, while other documents, because of their confidential nature, might need to be protected differently.

- **Personnel file**—This file should include the job description, application resume, offer letter, acknowledgement of organization handbook, emergency contact information, job performance, promotions, transfers, appraisals, awards, training, any disciplinary actions, and all documents related to separation from the organization.
- **Confidential personnel information**—These records should have an added layer of protection because of the employee's privacy rights and, if these rights are breached, to protect the employer from liability. These records usually include any medical information such as ADA accommodations, workers' compensation, drug tests, disability information, Family and Medical Leave Act (FMLA) information, health insurance, COBRA information, all employee credit information, I-9 form, and any documents related to a complaint or investigation.

Workplace policy should describe specifically where records will be stored and in what format—paper or electronic. Records should be held in a secure, locked location or electronically maintained with necessary technological protections. There is no specific law that dictates how records must be stored, whether paper or electronic, but the law does dictate that an organization must have the ability to quickly retrieve information and supply paper copies if necessary.

It is imperative for HR to always protect employee records and the privacy of the information, regardless of the format. Frequently, an organization will have a documented employee records confidentiality policy to protect all employee information and maintain confidentiality. Furthermore, if an employee feels there has been a breach in confidentiality, then HR needs to investigate the allegation immediately. Alternatively, if an organization feels there was a breach in confidentiality, regardless of how it occurred, the organization usually has an obligation to share the breach and offer corrective actions.

The pre-employment phase of a job comprises activities that occur before a candidate is chosen for and has accepted a position at an organization. During this phase, HR posts a job, resumes are submitted, applications are completed, reference checks and/or background checks may be conducted, and interviews may be held. All of these documents should be retained for EEO purposes demonstrating nondiscriminatory hiring, equal opportunity, and overall fairness and equity.

Organizations must retain the following information for all applicants: job posting; resumes; and completed applications, including interview notes related to the decision to hire or not hire an applicant. Based on federal regulations in the Age Discrimination in Employment Act (ADEA), Americans with Disabilities Act (ADA), and Civil Rights Act of 1964 (Title VII), these documents are retained one year after creation of the documents or hire/no-hire decision, whichever is later. In the case of federal contractors, document retention is two years. If the contractor has less than 150 employees or a government contract is less than $150,000, then the retention is, again, one year. These are the federal retention regulations, but retention rates could vary slightly depending on state and local laws.

- **Background checks**—These are retained for a minimum of one year based on the Equal Employment Opportunity Commission (EEOC) requirements and Title VII of the Civil Rights Act of 1964 to possibly report hiring and selection records. However, it is often recommended to save background check documents for five years after the date the consumer report is accessed because the statute of limitations in the Fair Credit Reporting Act is five years.
- **Tax records**—All related tax records should be retained by the employer for four years after the fourth quarter of the year in order to be in compliance with the Federal Insurance Contributions Act (FICA), Federal Unemployment Tax Act, and Internal Revenue Code.
- **Safety records**—This data, and related reports, should be retained for five years after the year that the record pertains to, based on the Occupational Safety and Health Act (OSHA) and the Walsh-Healey Act (for federal contractors).
- **Family and Medical Leave Act (FMLA) records**—Based on the requirements in the FMLA, these records should be retained for three years.
- **Disability accommodations**—All employee disability and accommodations documentation should be retained for one year from the date of the record or last date of an action. However, for contractors and public employees, the records should be retained for two years. There are many laws that require compliance with disability issues, such as the American Disabilities Act as Amended (ADAAA), Executive Order 11246, and the Vietnam Era Veterans' Readjustment Assistance Act (VEVRAA).

Records retention can be a complex process. However, it is a critical HR function to support and protect an organization.

Discuss risk management and methods to gauge risk.

Define the term "cost-benefit analysis" and describe how it applies to HR.

Identify some of the specific information that should be included in an emergency action plan.

List some of the steps that employers can take to prepare for emergencies and natural disasters.

Summarize emergency evacuation procedures and emergency simulations.

Identify the four characteristics an effective safety and health management plan should have, according to OSHA.

Cost-benefit analysis is presented as a ratio that helps an organization determine how certain activities and related costs impact its profitability. The following formula calculates the cost-benefit ratio:

$$Cost/benefit\ ratio = \frac{Projected\ value\ of\ benefits}{Cost}$$

For example, if an HR department made the decision to participate in an employee program that resulted in a cost savings of $10,000, and the cost of the program was $2,000, then the cost-benefit ratio would be 5:1. HR typically performs cost-benefit analyses on a regular basis to justify continuing or ending a particular program or activity.

Risk management is a methodical approach an organization engages in to identify, target, and initiate steps to minimize threats that could negatively impact an organization's health, safety, security, and privacy. While employers must abide by all federal, state, and local laws and regulations, they also have an obligation to protect employees from risks that could seriously harm the company, negatively impact morale, or create a financial burden. A **cost-benefit analysis**, or observing the potential cost of an endeavor against the benefit it will bring, is one of the methods an organization can utilize to evaluate risk. This type of evaluation relies on predicting the future based on available current information. Hence, there is an element of uncertainty with cost-benefit analysis that forces an organization to carefully examine all options and possible outcomes. Additionally, there are always unknowns in a situation, such as new obstacles or threats. Accordingly, there is a method to evaluate these risks called **enterprise risk management**. This methodology forces an organization to factor in those risks that have the highest likelihood of occurring, or whose impact is the most drastic. This allows organizations to strategically plan for worst-case scenarios and the possibility of perceived risks becoming realities.

Because it is an employer's obligation to provide a safe and healthy work environment, many companies have begun to create **emergency and disaster plans** for handling situations such as fires, explosions, earthquakes, chemical spills, communicable disease outbreaks, and acts of terrorism. These plans should include the following steps:

1. The **chain of command** should be clarified, and staff should be informed of who to contact and who has authority.
2. Someone should be responsible for **accounting** for all employees when an emergency occurs.
3. A **command center** should be set up to coordinate communications.
4. Employees should be **trained annually** on what to do if an emergency occurs.
5. Businesses should have **first-aid kits and basic medical supplies** available. This includes water fountains and eye wash stations in areas where spills may occur.
6. An **emergency team of employees** should be named and trained for the following:
   a. Organizing evacuation procedures
   b. Initiating shutdown procedures
   c. Using fire extinguishers
   d. Using oxygen and respirators
   e. Searching for disabled or missing employees
   f. Assessing when it is safe to re-enter the building

All emergency action plans should explain the alarm system that will be used to inform employees and other individuals at the worksite that they need to evacuate. They should also include in-depth exit route plans that describe which routes employees should take to escape the building, as well as in-depth plans that describe what actions employees should take before evacuating, such as shutting down equipment or closing doors. All emergency action plans should also include detailed systems for handling different types of emergencies and a system that can be used to verify that all employees have escaped the worksite.

According to the Occupational Safety and Health Administration (OSHA), there are four things a safety and health management plan should do to be considered effective:

- Establish a **specific system** that an organization can use to identify hazards in the workplace.
- Establish a **training program** that teaches employees to avoid hazards and perform tasks in the safest way possible.
- Include **specific procedures and programs** designed to eliminate hazards that the organization identifies, or at least minimize the risk that a hazard will injure or kill an employee or cause an employee to become ill.
- Allow employees at all levels of the organization to be **involved in the identification, prevention, and elimination** of hazards in the workplace.

Emergency evacuation procedures should be designed and developed according to the needs of the company to protect the business assets and the employees of the organization. Evacuation procedures should be comprehensive, covering preparations, building exit criteria, and the care and handling of vulnerable persons or employees who may be in danger. There should be highly visible maps of the building exits and designated employee meeting spots outside the building for accountability.

Emergency simulations that are practiced on a regular basis are critical elements of the evacuation plan. These simulations are more advanced than traditional fire drills or evacuation practices. Simulation runs have specific plans that are modeled on unique potential scenarios to which the team must respond. Responses are measured and scored to validate the plan, procedures, and systems, and are used to improve the plans. Simulations should be developed for many different scenarios to test each response plan.

Describe what is considered workplace violence and what actions an employer can do to address it.

Describe a business continuity plan and its five critical components.

Detail basic security concerns in a work environment.

Identify some of the specific information that should be included in a disaster recovery plan.

Summarize the importance of information technology (IT) security.

Explain what is meant by cybercrimes and what an organization can do to protect itself.

A business creates business continuity plans to ensure that the business can continue to operate in the face of a crisis or emergency that interferes with normal daily operations. When a disruption of daily operations occurs, the amount of time it takes for a business to recover data and resume normal operations and service is an indicator of whether that business has a well-planned continuity plan.
Business continuity plans consist of five critical components:

- A list of risks and an analysis of each risk's possible impact on the business
- A response plan for each risk
- Roles and responsibilities assigned for each response plan
- A communication plan to be implemented upon an event occurrence
- A training plan that is tested regularly

The business continuity plan should be fully developed and tested, and employees should all be trained on the implementation of the plan on a regular basis. Roles should be assigned and reviewed annually and when key employees leave the organization.

Workplace violence can be a physical act against someone, or it can be verbal abuse, threats, or intimidation. No matter what type, workplace violence is disturbing and dangerous, regardless of whether it is physical or psychological. There are numerous reasons why an employee may exhibit violent behavior, including a history of family abuse, drug or substance abuse, or mental illness. Workplace violence not only causes harm to the victim, but could also cause financial harm to a business, with damage to reputation possibly resulting in loss of clients, suppliers, or advertisers. Sometimes workplace violence is random and difficult to predict and prevent. However, there are steps an employer can take to reduce the chances of workplace violence:

- Establish a zero-tolerance policy against workplace violence that is documented and communicated to employees.
- Provide access to an employee assistance program (EAP) whereby employees can speak to a mental health counselor for referrals and appropriate treatment.
- Have only alcohol-free company events, possibly reducing the chances of workplace violence.
- Incorporate a violence prevention program into onboarding safety training.

Certain information should be included in every organization's disaster recovery plan. The plan should identify equipment and locations that can be utilized temporarily in the event of an emergency. It should also identify agencies and personnel that may be able to help the organization continue functioning immediately after an emergency. It is also wise to establish a set of procedures the organization can use to bring the personnel and equipment together after an emergency. Additionally, disaster recovery plans should identify alternative sources the organization can use to receive supplies or products if the emergency disables the organization's normal supply chain.

Employers have an obligation and a responsibility to keep employees and the work environment safe, and should have a security plan in place to help achieve that goal. This includes every contingency from a crisis to an uninvited visitor. A well-conceived security plan can reduce panic and enable employees to calmly respond to different types of crises. A security plan can include any or all of the following: photo badges, keycard access systems, locks on rooms and closets, an alarm system with backup, concealed alarms, visible and hidden cameras, exterior fencing and gates, exterior lighting, and security guards. Typically, security plans are designed with key management team members, including HR, to ensure the plan is comprehensive. Additionally, the security plan should highlight specific roles and backups in the event of a security breach. Having a security plan also helps to prevent panic in the event of a workplace emergency. Organizations should periodically review and practice planned drills to reinforce preparedness.

Cybercrime is when a computer or element of technology is used to commit an illegal act, such as violating privacy or stealing data, money, intellectual property, or identities. Cybercrime is a criminal activity even if the activity does not specifically involve money, for example, spreading viruses or causing other forms of technological harm. In fact, companies could be held liable if they do not impose actions or precautions to prevent cybercrimes from occurring. Furthermore, the financial cost of cybercrime to a business can be astronomical. The reality is that a large majority of work is completed with data and the transfer of data by employees. Therefore, it is extremely important for organizations to conduct background checks that include a look at the possibility of criminal hacking.

Employers should take steps to allow and promote open communication and report any suspected cybercrime the moment there is an indication that something might be wrong. Employers should communicate the importance of not opening anything via email or any other form of technology or software that could be linked to scams, hacking, phishing, etc. Companies should make every effort possible to protect their data, including not transferring data on unsecured or unencrypted servers, not posting company information on public social media sites, and updating antivirus protection software. An organization's best defense against cybercrime is vigilance in monitoring and taking every possible systemic precaution to protect its data.

IT security is becoming a more serious topic and rapidly gaining more attention. It is important for HR practitioners to be conscientious of controls to mitigate organizational exposure and risk. Some companies may have IT security policies and acknowledgements in place to identify and document compliance and security controls and to reduce liability. Multiple layers of corporate IT security might include the encryption of data files, firewalls, access controls or logins, systems monitoring, detection processes, antivirus software, and cyber insurance. Implementing stronger IT security can provide companies with benefits such as mitigating lost revenue, protecting brand reputation, and supporting mobilization.

Compliance and Risk Management
© Mometrix Media - flashcardsecrets.com/hrci
aPHR Exam

Describe theft and fraud in the workplace and measures an employer can take to prevent it from happening.

Compliance and Risk Management
© Mometrix Media - flashcardsecrets.com/hrci
aPHR Exam

Detail what steps can be taken by a company in the event of equipment damage or destruction.

Compliance and Risk Management
© Mometrix Media - flashcardsecrets.com/hrci
aPHR Exam

Describe how an organization can minimize password breach risks.

Compliance and Risk Management
© Mometrix Media - flashcardsecrets.com/hrci
aPHR Exam

List some guidelines that should be considered when drafting a password policy.

Compliance and Risk Management
© Mometrix Media - flashcardsecrets.com/hrci
aPHR Exam

Explain corporate espionage between companies.

Compliance and Risk Management
© Mometrix Media - flashcardsecrets.com/hrci
aPHR Exam

Describe the purpose of downsizing and its impact on an organization.

Company equipment is typically provided to employees to efficiently perform the functions of their job. Equipment provided can include laptops, printers, cell phones, or cars. Over time, and for various reasons, equipment can be damaged or destroyed. This hurts a company both monetarily and timewise, via work disruption. There are policies and steps an organization can take to mitigate equipment damage or destruction. To begin, companies should have an equipment property policy. This policy should reinforce that all equipment provisioned to or used by employees is the property of the company and is to be used only for company purposes. There should be a procedure in place of who to notify, and when, in the event that equipment is damaged, lost, stolen, or destroyed. The policy should also state disciplinary actions that could occur if the damage was due to negligence.

Employers should consult all federal, state, and local laws and regulations, as they vary from state to state, with regard to recovering lost expenses for equipment. Additionally, if equipment is damaged or destroyed due to unforeseen conditions such as fire, water, or disaster, companies should consult their insurance policy and/or other federal, state, and local resources.

Theft and fraud in the workplace are extremely costly to an organization, and every effort should be made to prevent them. **Theft** is when property or information is taken without consent. **Fraud** is when some form of deception is utilized to take something for personal gain. Fraud is a form of theft. Employees may steal for any number of reasons: a sense of entitlement, the belief that they are underpaid, because it was easy, and more. Furthermore, theft could include almost anything that belongs to the company. Common types of theft include cash, products, equipment, services, ideas, and data. Fraud is a variation of theft and could include inflation of expense accounts, falsified payrolls, fabricated receipts, unrecorded vacation or personal time, forgeries, entertainment expenses without a legitimate link to a business purpose, or fictitious purchase orders.

Regardless of why or what is stolen, theft and fraud are illegal, and should be investigated by the company if suspected. To help prevent theft and fraud, organizations should consider doing the following:
- Conduct background checks on employees before hiring.
- Maintain an inventory control system (if applicable).
- Establish and communicate an employee theft policy, including consequences if found guilty after an investigation.
- Install security cameras (if appropriate).

The following are some guidelines that could be adopted while drafting a password policy:
- Passwords should be strong, complex, and challenging for someone to guess—typically they should be combinations of uppercase letters, lowercase letters, numbers, punctuation marks, and special characters, and preferably over eight characters long. Passwords should not be obvious or easy to determine. For instance, Password123! would be a poor password.
- Default passwords, those given by IT for various reasons, should be changed immediately after logging in.
- Passwords should not be shared with anyone. If this occurs, then the employee should change the password immediately.
- Employers should educate employees on ways to avoid phishing scams that might be used to steal passwords.
- To prevent discovery, passwords should be neither written down nor stored in an employee's workspace.

Passwords are needed for almost every program that is opened on a computer, and it is critical to develop and maintain them in such a way as to minimize risk to the company. Many companies have developed password policies to help manage the process and ensure it is being monitored and enforced with regularity. Most password policies are developed with the whole life cycle of the password in mind, including the creation of passwords, the interval of time at which they are changed, and guidelines for the prevention of password theft. Research indicates that data breaches involving passwords are more likely to occur with a phishing attack or someone inside the company getting knowledge about passwords—as when passwords are left out on a drawer or written on a piece of paper—than by outside hacking.

Downsizing, sometimes referred to as "workforce reduction," is a strategically planned and necessary elimination of jobs in order to make an organization potentially more competitive and ideally more profitable. This process is intended to reduce operating costs for the purpose of maximizing production, which is intended to drive profitability in a positive direction. Downsizing can occur for any number of reasons, including a decrease in profits over a period of time, closure in parts or entire lines of the business, or acquisitions that might involve duplication of functions. Downsizing is not linked to employee performance and is usually regarded as a complex process due to all the factors that must be taken into consideration.

Organizations need to identify exactly what downsizing will achieve, create reliable and legally defensible selection criteria, develop a plan for work redistribution (if applicable), and gauge how downsizing will impact the business in the short and long term. Typically, the process of downsizing negatively impacts both productivity and morale. Hence, the employer should communicate with employees throughout the process and keep the lines of two-way communication open in order to minimize disruption to the business.

Corporate espionage is a type of spying between companies that involves taking some type of information that would provide one with an unfair advantage over the other. This type of secret could be (but is not limited to) trade secrets or a competitor's plans for future products, services or endeavors, or strategic plans. Corporate espionage can range from a disgruntled employee leaving a company for a competitor and sharing some type of secret, to hacking into or launching malware on a competitor's system. Obtaining information about competitors is not always a crime. For example, a retail company could send secret shoppers to a competitor's retail company to evaluate how they perform specific functions. In this case, they are obtaining information in a legally acceptable manner. However, intentionally (and often, deceptively) obtaining a trade secret without the owner's consent is not legal. Evaluating legality in corporate espionage is extremely complex. The federal Economic Espionage Act of 1996 essentially makes it illegal to steal commercial secrets. For those found guilty, financial penalties could be severe, possibly including prison time. Additionally, violators could be subject to civil litigation. Some states have even more stringent laws and regulations to combat corporate espionage.

Describe some options a company can explore before implementing a downsizing plan.

List the first four steps for a reduction in force (RIF) needed in order to downsize.

List the last three steps for a reduction in force (RIF) needed in order to downsize.

Summarize the role of outplacement firms.

Explain the difference between a merger and an acquisition.

Describe what is meant by a divestiture, and explain some of the reason why a company would take such an action.

The following are the steps for conducting a layoff or reduction in force (RIF):

1. Select employees for layoff using seniority, performance, job classification, location, or skill.
2. Ensure selected employees do not affect a protected class to avoid adverse or disparate impact.
3. Review compliance with federal and state WARN Act regulations, which require employers to provide 60 days' notice to affected employees while specifying whether the reduction in force is permanent or for a specified amount of time.
4. Review compliance with the Older Workers Benefit Protection Act, which provides workers over the age of 40 the opportunity to review any severance agreements that require their waiver of discrimination claims. The act allows a consideration period of 21 days if only one older worker is being separated, and 45 days when two or more older workers are being separated. They also must receive a revocation period of seven days after signing the agreement. Additionally, they must be informed of the positions and ages of the other employees affected by the layoffs so that they can assess whether or not they feel age discrimination has taken place.

The decision to downsize is rarely an easy one. However, it is often a necessity for a business to stay viable. The negative effect of downsizing on a business culture and its brand in the marketplace is challenging. Therefore, many businesses look for alternatives to downsizing before implementing a reduction in force. Some of these alternatives include the following:

- Implement an immediate **hiring freeze** and work with employees on work redistribution if needed.
- Reduce employees' hours.
- Create an **early retirement program**, whereby the company can offer eligible employees financial incentives to leave. Eligibility can be tied to years of service and/or age to incentivize the most senior employees to take early retirement.
- **Reduce pay** in order to avoid layoffs, although the employer must pay careful attention to legal regulations and consistency in implementation.
- Place employees on **furloughs** if the financial distress is temporary.
- Encourage employees to **voluntarily leave with incentives**, which could include a generous severance package and/or outplacement services.

An **outplacement firm** is an external vendor that is contracted by an organization in the event the organization needs to reduce its workforce and lay off a large number of employees—sometimes referred to as a "reduction in force" (RIF). Outplacement firms, sometimes called career transition services, offer services to outgoing employees to cope with the loss of a job and assist in finding a new job. Usually, outplacement firms are contracted and paid for by the organization that is laying off its employees. This service is typically part of an employee severance benefit and is therefore offered at no cost to the exiting employee.

Services provided by an outplacement firm can vary, but some of the most common offerings are career assessments, career coaching, job search programs, and resume and networking workshops. Depending on the options selected by the organization, services can be in-person, one-on-one, group, and/or video appointments. An organization may choose to utilize the services of an outplacement firm because it is the moral or conscientious and responsible thing to do, because it may reduce the risk of litigation, or because it protects the employer's reputation by assisting their displaced employees.

The following are the steps for conducting a layoff or reduction in force (RIF):

1. Determine if severance packages, including salary continuation, vacation pay, employer-paid COBRA premiums, outplacement services, or counseling, might be available to affected employees. Typically, employees laid off in a RIF will sign a document called a separation and general release, whereby the employee signing the document accepts a severance package and agrees to not sue or make any claims against a company. A company is never required to offer a severance package.
2. When conducting meetings with employees, be empathetic, have tissues, ensure that all required documentation is available to the employee, and review all information in detail.
3. Inform the current workforce by communicating sustainability concerns, methods used to determine who would be selected for the reduction in force, and commitment to meeting company goals and objectives to maintain morale and productivity.

A **divestiture** is the opposite of an acquisition, whereby a company separates a portion of itself, usually a division or subsidiary, in a form of restructuring.

A company that initiates a divestiture typically seeks to remove a business line that is unrelated to its core operations or is simply a poor fit that requires inordinate management attention. A subsidiary that operates in an aging business with modest growth prospects may be sold or spun off in order to focus on more promising opportunities.

Alternatively, the divestment may be required by a regulatory authority, such as to comply with an antitrust adjudication.

During a divestiture process, it is critical to update the business continuity plan for the organization. As elements of the business are separated from the core and sold off or removed and data is separated, workflows are adapted, processes are changed, and employees are moved out and around the company, it will be critical to readdress the risks, requirements, and roles and responsibilities that have been altered and rework and reassign them. In the event of an emergency, the transitioning company cannot afford to have a lack of plans that could result in a failure in service or the inability to reconstitute the organization.

During the divestiture process, the business continuity plan should be reviewed, updated, rewritten, and tested, and employees trained, as quickly as possible during the transitioning of the company.

Mergers and acquisitions are similar in many ways, as both terms refer to a type of structural change in which two organizations join together to form a single organization. However, the two terms refer to different ways in which an organization's structure changes. A **merger** refers to a situation in which two or more organizations agree to combine into a single organization because both organizations will benefit from the merger. An **acquisition**, on the other hand, refers to a situation in which an organization purchases enough of another organization's stock to take control of the organization's operations. This is an important difference because all of the organizations involved in a merger must agree to the merger, while the organizations involved in an acquisition do not necessarily need to agree to the acquisition in order for it to take place.

The most vulnerable time period of a merger or acquisition is the transition through the first year, when roles and responsibilities are still being sorted out, employees are feeling vulnerable, and emotions are typically running high. With this in mind, it is critical that a new business continuity plan be created during the process of defining organizational structure.

As executives are seated in new roles, the management staff is shuffled and reassigned, and organizations are realigned, the team responsible for the business continuity plan must work closely with the teams to reassess the plan and the roles and responsibilities, and to develop a new communication plan. The executives must be briefed on the new business continuity plan, and once it is approved, it must be rolled out to employees, who must be trained, and the plan must be tested.

If a crisis or emergency occurs during the transition time frame or within the first few years of merger or acquisition activity, and a business continuity plan has not been very clearly defined, roles have not been assigned, and plans have not been tested, the organization will be at high risk for failure.